The N̶ ⋮

A Crit ⋮

nation

By Jonathan M.S. Pearce

The Nativity: A Critical Examination
Copyright © 2012 Jonathan M.S. Pearce
Reprinted 2013

Published by *Onus Books*

Printed by Lightning Source International

All rights reserved. No part of this publication may be reproduced, stored in a retrieval system, or transmitted in any form by any means, electronic, mechanical, photocopy, recording, or otherwise, without the prior permission of the publisher, except as provided for by UK copyright law.

Cover design: Onus Books

Scripture taken from the NEW AMERICAN STANDARD BIBLE®, Copyright ©1960, 1962, 1963, 1968, 1971, 1972, 1973, 1975, 1977, 1995 by The Lockman Foundation. Used by permission. All rights reserved.

Trade paperback ISBN: 978-0-9566948-5-0

OB 01/05

About the author:

Jonathan M.S. Pearce is a teacher and author from south Hampshire, UK, who has dedicated many years to studying all manner of things philosophical and theological. Whilst studying for a Masters in Philosophy from the University of Wales, Trinity St. David (he also holds a degree from the University of Leeds, and a Post Graduate Certificate of Education from St. Mary's University College, London), he became a founder member of the Skeptic Ink Network (SIN). This group of authors, academics and activists offer the freethought community a fantastic resource of writing and critical content (Pearce's blog, A Tippling Philosopher can be found at www.skepticink.com/tippling). As a founder member of the Tippling Philosophers, a friendly group of disparate believers and non-believers, and sort-of believers, based in Hampshire, he is a big advocate of casual philosophy groups meeting over pints of good ale. He lives with his partner and twin boys and wonders how she puts up with him.

This is his fourth book, after writing *Free Will? An investigation into whether we have free will, or whether I was always going to write this book,* a popular philosophy, science and theology book looking into the age-old free will vs. determinism debate. He has also written *The Little Book of Unholy Questions*, a set of questions directly asked to God which looks to show the incoherence of the idea of an all-loving, all-knowing and all-powerful God. As an interlude from writing about philosophy and theology, he has branched out by writing a book of advice for dads of twins, *Twins: A Survival Guide for Dads.* They need all the help they can get.

*To the Tippling Philosophers
and casual thinkers everywhere.*

A note about the book:

There is much research to cram into some short pages. Therefore, I have had to be very concise with some of my conclusions. I have made great use of Gerd Theissen and Annette Merz's work *The Historical Jesus* because it is a summary of the research on the historical Jesus from both sides of the fence. I have found it to be a most useful reference tool.

There is also plenty of reference to the excellent *The Birth of the Messiah* by Raymond Brown, the great Catholic biblical scholar. This provides a good, even, and in places, critical look at the nativity narratives. I have also used Charles Foster's 2007 book *The Christmas Mystery* as it provides an interesting exposé of how a liberal Christian deals with the incongruities of the infancy stories. There are many other references in this book as it is vital to pull on as many fields of expertise as possible to reach solid conclusions. Richard Carrier's work, both online and in written format, provides some excellent critical analysis.

As ever, there are many sections which require further reading. Some subjects receive a more cursory analysis since there are some very involved arguments on either side. For example, Jesus' comparative similarities to Mithras have been well documented over the years, but have also received heavy criticism from within and without the Christian academic world. As a result, I deemed it unnecessary to include too much on this. I leave it up to the readers to further any such research and make up their own conclusions.

For Bible translations, the New American Standard Bible translation is used for all of the biblical quotes. I have always found this to be a really good translation because it is literal whilst being readable. It does not fall into the trap that some modern translations do of changing words or phrases to be more politically correct and easier on the eye and mind for some readers. I find this tantamount to propaganda! I do not always mark the verses but I will reference them so that the text reads more fluidly. On occasion, for reference purposes, I do mark the verses.

Each section deserves a book in its own right and I hope I have done justice to summing up vast areas of historical and textual research as concisely and informatively as possible.

A reprint of this book took place in 2013 to change typographical issues and suchlike.

Acknowledgements:

A great many thanks, as ever, are due to a great many people. Firstly, Saga Sabin all the way over in Canada has been very helpful for editorial comments. She and other members of the multinational 'B.A.S.H.' group have been great friends and great minds to bounce things off. From Brazil to Sweden, Canada to the U.S., technology makes things so cosy and easy these days! Thanks must also go to Sergio Paulo Sider for adding valuable comments to questions and musings.

Edward T. Babinski, author of *Leaving the Fold*, yet again, has been an enthusiastic contributor of sources and ideas.

Thanks also to Ben Wilson for pointers and advice—it is always welcome.

Finally, a huge thanks to David Fitzgerald for the foreword and for useful editorial advice and information with regard to certain sections.

However, any editorial mistakes are entirely my own.

Contents

Foreword

It's one thing to reject the Gospel accounts because they don't pass the Smell Test. That is to say, since they are filled with patently supernatural elements (Divine messengers from heaven, choirs of angels, fiery portents in the sky, etc.), standard legendary events (a tyrant slaying innocents, a woman impregnated by a deity, prophets announcing the arrival of the Messiah, et al.) and even the more mundane and plausible elements completely uncorroborated in the contemporary historical record, we can probably safely file them away with all the rest of the stories of miracle-working demigods from the ancient world: if it looks like a myth, sounds like a myth, and reads like a myth... chances are better than decent that it *is* a myth.

And in virtually every single case of supernatural figures found in the pages of ancient history, both religious and secular readers are perfectly comfortable with making that very judgment—except for one. Jesus of Nazareth, though he shares much in common with his fellow demigods, miracle-workers and prophets, somehow gets a pass. All the others—they were all no more than myths, legends and stories, but now, Jesus—*that* was different. But is it, really?

Jonathan M.S. Pearce has put his money (and his mind) where his mouth is, and done the hard work of actually taking these claims seriously enough to put them under the microscope and keenly, methodically examining not only the texts themselves, but also taking on the seemingly endless armory-worth of arguments, defenses and obfuscations thrown up by apologists in their efforts to shore up and fortify a position that ultimately, cannot even stand on its own. The Nativity Story, like so many elements that comprise the accounts of Jesus' life, ministry, death and resurrection, simply crumbles under its own weight.

It's striking to realize first of all that of our four allegedly biographical sources for Jesus, two fail to mention his birth at all, and strikingly don't support the idea that there was anything unusual or noteworthy about his birth at all. What's worse, the two sources that that do present his nativity are both taken from our first, no-frills gospel of Mark. Fully 50% of Mark is repro-

1

duced in Luke, a whopping 90% in Matthew. They took Mark's basic story (copying it largely verbatim) and each then expanded on it with their own additions—which, as we'll soon see, are completely incompatible with one another. John, for his part, doesn't bother trying to correspond with the earlier gospels - his Jesus *doesn't even get crucified on the same day.* So when our four "biographical sources" are not all in lockstep, they are in diametric opposition—ironic, considering that the original gospel (Mark 3:25) puts these words in Jesus' mouth: "If a house is divided against itself, that house will not be able to stand." It's a discovery that has caused more than a few biblical historians to cast serious doubt of the reliability of the gospels.

But don't take my word for it. Read Jonathan Pearce's case and decide for yourself.

David Fitzgerald

Author of *Nailed: Ten Christian Myths That Show Jesus Never Existed at All*

San Francisco, May 9th, 2012

Introduction

It's an annual ritual. A cultural showcase paying homage to our religious heritage. A moment of familial pride. A period of tension for worried teachers. Yes, it is that time of year, the Christmas musical extravaganza that is the school nativity. We've all been there, as child, parent, grandparent or teacher, looking on with some kind of deep-seated emotion. In an era of shifting sands of culture and religion, it remains a fairly stalwart date in the academic calendar.

Aside from its position as a cultural phenomenon and an opportunity to film and photograph your loved ones to later embarrass them when they are famous, what is this story that the children work so hard to replay?

In simple terms, this is the birth of God, incarnated in man-form. In order to pay for the sins of humanity (and there is much debate over the finer details here), God needed some kind of compensation. As a result, he sacrificed himself to, well, himself, in order to atone for these sins.

The nativity play, however, is always a case of smashing together two stories like two separate oceans thrusting into each other, only to mingle inseparably, losing their own identity.

This is because there are two sources for the nativity story: two out of the four Gospels report it. Now, for people less knowledgeable of the Bible (and this refers to Christians and non-Christians alike), the nativity story is *not* a universally reported story in the Gospels. This itself presents a potential issue. More importantly, though, is the notion that the two Gospel accounts that there are (Luke and Matthew) do not agree with each other on details, and those which they claim mean that it is very difficult to get them to cohere with each other.

So when, for example, the children in the play act as Joseph, Mary and the donkey traipsing across the countryside to attend a census, one sees reference to the Gospel of Luke. However, when a surly child takes on the famous role of Herod demanding all sorts of evils, we see reference to the Gospel of Matthew. As we shall see later, there is immense problem in reconciling these two pieces of information (the census and Herod) into one coherent story. The popular understanding of the nativity, then, is a splicing of these two disparate narratives. Matthew and Luke are both invariably seen as being veracious (in part or wholly) and are both often seen as being able to be woven into a single narrative.

The purpose of this book, then, is to question whether this is an honest and reasonable approach to take—to take both accounts as 'Gospel' truth, and to weave them together. Or even, for that matter, to take either of them as representing a historical truth.

Now it may come as some surprise to many less critical readers of the Bible, but there are many *Christian* scholars who conclude that the narratives which describe the birth of Jesus are not the most accurate accounts in history. The scholars of the period of Higher Criticism in the 18th and 19th centuries started the ball rolling, with academics such as D.F. Strauss making assertions of mythology with regard to the birth narratives. More recently, respected Catholic scholar Raymond E. Brown has cast some serious doubt over the historicity of the accounts, along with a whole host of others, such as E.P. Sanders and Gerd Theissen.[1]

This does prompt the question as to how reliable the accounts are if many good scholars within the disciplines of New Testament study doubt the veracity of these accounts of the infancy narratives. And when the work of secular and more critical scholars is taken into account, it can be argued that the narratives start crumbling. This is what I will be arguing.

If, indeed, the accounts supplied by the authors of Luke and Matthew are somewhat dubious in their historicity, where does this leave us? And more importantly, where does it leave the Christian who adheres to the notion of a historical Jesus and the incarnation of God on earth? If there is doubt about these historical claims, what, then, are the authors trying to say and what evidence *do* they muster to support such claims? That is something which I will look at in the conclusion to this work.

---

[1] *The Historical Jesus: A Comprehensive Guide* by Gerd Theissen (1998), for example, details scholarship across the board and casts doubt on the historicity of the accounts from multiple angles.

4

I have endeavoured to strike a balance between a scholarly approach to this work as well as hoping that it will appeal to the popular reader interested in reading about one of the cornerstones of Christianity. There will be footnotes, but I will keep them on the relevant page so as to avoid the need to flip back and forth. I have divided up the arguments into some twenty points, some of which may contain a few more critical lines of reasoning. These arguments, add up to a cumulative case that does, in my opinion, lead to the inevitable conclusion that the infancy narratives are (at least mainly) fictional. It seems to me that, though the cumulative case seems to be water-tight, even looking at some of the individual points on their own merit, one can cast huge doubt on the whole of the historical claim.

With each point, I have tried to include all the relevant counter-points and claims which apologists have come up with, in order to present a fair and balanced case. Hopefully, this means that I am not committing a straw man fallacy and presenting a criticism against these accounts which can be and has been answered. Having said this, it is apparent to me, at least, that in order continue to hold the Gospel narratives to be true and accurate, some of these counter-claims are incredibly ad hoc and spurious in their own historical defensibility and sheer believability.

This book is aimed both at Christians and at non-Christians for fairly obvious reasons. Firstly, there are many Christians who are unfamiliar with critical scholarship, or who like to be critical themselves, and this offers the opportunity to find out the arguments contrary to their faith so that they can make their belief as rigorous as possible, or even to find that it does not stand up well enough to the rigours of critical analysis. For the non-believer or non-Christian it can be seen as ammunition for a cumulative case against the historicity of (at least parts of) the Bible and the religious claims of the Christian faith. I am seeking to pull all of the arguments about the nativity into one place.

Christmas nativities are wonderful occasions for proud parents and they can still remain that way. Most plays acted out around theatres are either fictional, have true themes or are based on a mere nugget of truth. The Christmas nativity can simply join that long list of great works.

5

PART 1 – THE GOSPEL ACCOUNTS

Introduction to the texts

It would be imprudent to start talking about the issues with the textual accounts of the nativity without at first acknowledging their background and discussing the state of play with regard to their historical and textual pedigree.

Much of what I say may already be common knowledge to some of the readers, and yet to others it may be new territory. Let us start by looking at the context of all of the Gospels in order to determine something about the who, what, where and why of the texts.

As with everything biblical, there is a spectrum of approaches to the interpretation of the texts; who wrote them and when they were written, as well as what type of texts they are, for what reasons they were committed to 'paper' and whether they represent historical fact or religious symbolism. Quite often in biblical exegesis (the study and interpretation of texts) scholars are prone to starting with a conclusion and then massaging or searching for evidence that supports that conclusion, as opposed to surveying all the evidence, piecing it together and seeing in what direction it takes them. One should build a conclusion from the brickwork of evidence rather than vice-versa.

The general consensus amongst scholars is that the Gospels were written by non-eyewitnesses. That means that the people who are giving us arguably the only sources of information about Jesus never actually met him. To make matters worse, the Gospel of Mark (if one assumes Markan priority which means that Mark was written first) was generally thought to have been written about forty to fifty years after the death of Jesus (around 70 CE), probably in Syria.[1] As such, all of the other Gospels were written later, and most probably in other countries, using the lingua franca, Greek, and not the native tongue of Jesus, Aramaic.

It is also generally thought that Mark, along with an unknown source (called Q by modern scholars), provided the source material for the Gospels of Luke and Matthew, although there is some debating of this by recent scholars such as Mark Goodacre. The implications of there being no Q are interesting since, if this is correct, it seems that the parts that do overlap (Q) are actually instances where Luke has copied Matthew (who reworked Mark). Thus the Gospels are even less independent. As David Fitzgerald expounded in *Nailed: Ten Christian Myths That Show Jesus Never Existed At All* (p. 67):

> The three share a truly astonishing number of near-identical passages, arranged in much the same order and in many cases using the exact same wording. Luke reproduces 50% of Mark's text, and Matthew a whopping 90%. Of the 661 verses in Mark's Gospel, Luke's Gospel uses about 360 and Matthew's Gospel uses about 607.4 The parallels are so widespread and apparent that the majority opinion among Biblical authorities has been in agreement ever since; namely that Matthew and Luke based their material upon Mark's. If the Farrer or Goodacre Hypotheses are correct (and I believe Goodacre's modified Farrer hypothesis is), Luke also copied from Matthew (while others speculate both used a hypothetical second source, "Q").

The names 'Matthew, Mark, Luke and John' were names later ascribed to the writings by early church fathers but modern scholars rarely believe that the names have any real relevance to the authors of the works.

It is essentially unclear what the sources for Mark were, but it is assumed they included a mixture of certainly oral and possibly written pieces of sayings of Jesus, the passion narrative (Easter Story), some miracle stories and so on.[2]

---

[1] Theissen (1998) p 24-27

[2] Ibid.

What interests me is how there are so many examples of speech in the Bible, particularly the New Testament, and often passages of speech to which there were probably no witnesses (Jesus talking to Herod) available to the Gospel writers. All these speeches seem to have been remarkably well-preserved considering the people listening would most likely have been illiterate or certainly did not have notebooks or Dictaphones handy. This raises the question as to the authenticity of the direct speech reported in the Gospels, and whether these speeches were historically factual.

Furthermore, there are situations whereby there can only have been one or two actual eyewitnesses to an event reported. However, and even if one assumes that the eyewitnesses survived the forty years until the Gospels were written (given low life expectancies), there are differences and discrepancies in the accounts that should not be there given that the original source must have been the same person or few people. An example might be the empty tomb narratives whereby different people were claimed to have been present, one reporting one angel, and another reporting two and a third reporting none. If modern newspapers were reporting an event in which all witnesses saw, say, two angels, you can guarantee that all the papers would agree on that one main fact given the extraordinary claim.

So the situation we have is that these accounts of Jesus were written by unknown people in essentially unknown places, and at a time we can only make good guesses at. None of the Gospels detail their sources as you would expect from good historians. Some earlier and contemporaneous historians to the Gospel writers such as Thucydides, Polybius and Arrian included some of their sources, and some of the lesser historians such as Suetonius did so too. These vital references to sources are missing in the case of all the Gospel accounts. This essentially means that the verifiability of the events which are claimed to have happened is nigh on impossible.

Another problem with assessing the historicity of the Gospels is knowing which passages are reporting historical fact and which are written as symbolic passages; allegories to put forward a particular theme. In 2011 renowned New Testament scholar Mike Licona was forced to resign from his teaching post and position as research professor of New Testament at Southern

Evangelical Seminary and was ousted as apologetics coordinator for the North America Mission Board. This was because, in one of his books *The Resurrection of Jesus: A New Historiographical Approach*, he examined a passage in Matthew 27 which reports resurrected saints parading around Jerusalem. In researching this passage, Licona came up with a theory which annoyed the biblical literalist camp. The problem is that there is no other evidence to support this extraordinary biblical claim. As Licona said, "Based on my reading of the Greco-Roman, Jewish, and biblical litera-ture, I proposed that the raised saints are best interpreted as Matthew's use of an apocalyptic symbol communicating that the Son of God had just died."[1] Because he was bucking a conservative trend of not reading the passage literally, he had to go as his colleagues and peers were more literal in their understanding of the text. This just shows that one scholar can read an account as being symbolic whilst another concludes antithetically. This will come into play later in the book as I look at whether or not the birth narratives have a symbolic overlay to heighten the impor-tance of what was probably a very ordinary birth to compete with other myths and religions of the era as well as with a Roman Emperor.

Another issue with the Gospels in general is the fact that they are not attested by extra-biblical sources. This means that no other source outside of the Bible, and contemporary with the events or with the Gospel accounts, reports and corroborates the events claimed within the Gospels. Theists make much out of what is mentioned in extra-biblical sources such as Josephus, Tacitus, Suetonius and so on but all that these sources can vali-date (when they are not shown to be interpolations or edited additions) is that Christians, who followed Christ, existed. Not really the greatest of conclusions.

Archaeology doesn't particularly support the accounts of a historical Jesus, or any of his Apostles.[2] There are some events

---

[1] Interpretation Sparks a Grave Theology Debate by bobby Ross Jnr., Christianity Today,
http://www.christianitytoday.com/ct/2011/november/interpretation-sparks-theology-debate.html (retrieved 12/2011)
[2] E.H. Cline (2009) in *Biblical Archaeology: A Very Short Introduction (Very Short Introductions)*, p. 103

and places referred to which are of course verified, but that amounts to the analogy of the places and events of Victorian London being mentioned in Sherlock Holmes by Conan Doyle being real; it in no way follows that Sherlock Holmes was a real historical figure.

A further problem is that the accounts were written by people with a vested interest in seeing the life and teachings of Jesus evangelised to those in the world around them. One might question the reliability, for example, of a biography of David Koresh or Sathya Sai Baba (and the many miracles his followers have claimed of him) if it were written by their most fervent of followers. People who believe after the time of some such events that they were miraculous will create accounts of those events which might not reflect their true nature, ex post facto. In this way, the Gospel writers, without knowing Jesus, come to believe that he was resurrected and carried out miracles (without witnessing them) and then go on to write his biography with those beliefs firmly embedded. Are we in a position to truly trust these sources, given the magnitude of their claims and the biases which they must obviously have? These claims purportedly prove (or strongly evidence) certain supposed events which the authors themselves did not witness.

This brings me on to a certain maxim which was popularised by Carl Sagan, but which already existed in some form or other since the philosophising of David Hume, the Scottish Enlightenment philosopher. Sagan, the popular scientist who died in 1996 claimed that "Extraordinary claims require extraordinary evidence."[1] This is a self-evidently true maxim, even though many theists seek to deny its power. This is because they misunderstand its best application. This claim is a statement which is most aptly applied to secondary or tertiary evidence. Let me exemplify what I mean, by way of five claims and how most people would assess them:

Claim 1: *I have a dog.*
Nothing more than verbal testimony needed.

---

[1] "Encyclopaedia Galactica". Carl Sagan (writer/host). *Cosmos*. PBS. December 14, 1980. No. 12. 01:24 minutes in.

Claim 2: *I have a dog which is in the bath.*
As above, with one eyebrow raised.

Claim 3: *I have a dog in the bath wearing a dress.*
I would probably need a photo of this to believe you.

Claim 4: *I have a dress-wearing dog in the bath with a skunk wearing a SCUBA outfit.*
I would need some video evidence at the least

Claim 5: *I have the above in the bath, but the bath water is boiling and the animals are happy.*
I would need video and independent attestation that the video was not doctored agreeing that this is what appeared to be happening.

Claim 6: *All of the above, but the dog has a fire-breathing dragon on its shoulder and the skunk is dancing with a live unicorn.*
Well I'll be damned, I'll need video, plus video of the video, plus independent attestation from multiple recognisably reliable sources, and assessment and evaluation by technological experts and biological experts, plus a psychological evaluation of the claimant, and so on etc.

The point of this exercise is to show that when evaluating evidence that is not first-hand we have different criteria for assessing its veracity, depending on the type of claim. It is actually all about probability: claims which are highly improbable require a great deal of evidence, even if they are physically (naturalistically) possible claims. The claim that I climbed Mount Everest without using my right arm, and only one eye, is of something which is physically possible but ultimately very unlikely. As a result, people would naturally demand more evidence than me merely telling them in a casual conversation. The more improbable my claim, the more incredible; the more incredible, the higher the demands for evidence. This is just intuitive. If we then make a claim which is about as unlikely as can possibly be: that a man-God dies and is resurrected (or commits any of his miracles), then these claims are of events which defy the laws of nature as we know them. This is, almost by definition, the most improbable set of claims. As a result, they should demand the highest level of evidence, especially when not witnessed first-hand.

If we look at Matthew 27:51-53, we can put this into context:

> And behold, the veil of the temple was torn in two from top to bottom; and the earth shook and the rocks were split. The tombs were opened, and many bodies of the saints who had fallen asleep were raised; and coming out of the tombs after His resurrection they entered the holy city and appeared to many.

This is a truly miraculous and improbable claim. The passage claims that at the death of Jesus, the saints rose out of their tombs, being a host of resurrected bodies, and paraded around Jerusalem. What is the evidence that we have in order to judge whether this claim is veracious or not? An anonymously written non-eyewitness account produced some decades after the event by a fervent follower and evangeliser that is unverifiable and some 2000 years old. Even stranger is the fact that these publicly resurrected saints appeared to "many" in Jerusalem and yet we have no other accounts of this event, no corroboration from any other source—and this would have been the most amazing sight in any of the witnesses' lives. We *should* apply the criteria that extraordinary claims require extraordinary evidence for the reasons mentioned. This is an event which patently demands such treatment and it has only very poor evidence to support it. As a result, this claim should be discarded as either false or highly dubious. At the very best, I would recommend agnosticism over its verisimilitude.

I am sure that you can imagine what comes next. If we substitute Matthew 27 with the miraculous accounts of Jesus' birth, then we are left with the same conclusion. However, I will save such an analysis for later. Suffice to say that the level of evidence provided by the Gospels, as a whole, is poor, and most likely not good enough to satisfy the probabilities of the claims being made therein.

One final point to make before looking at the two accounts individually is made very well by the great Raymond E. Brown in *The Birth of the Messiah* (p.35):

> But if originally there was one narrative, how did it ever become fragmented into the two different accounts we have now? As I hinted above, the suggestion that Matthew is giving Joseph's remembrance of the events, while Luke is giving Mary's, is just a pious deduction from the fact that Joseph dominates Matthew's account, and Mary dominates Luke's. In point of fact, how could Joseph ever have told the story in Matthew and not have reported the annunciation of Mary? And how could Mary have been responsible for the story in Luke and never have mentioned the coming of the magi and the flight to Egypt?

This is so crucial and well put by Brown. How, indeed, could a singular, linear account of the events of the nativity become divided? Why, especially if the sources were the same or at least very close to each other? What is a better explanation of this fact: that the events were later made up by the Gospel writers; or some other ad hoc and harmonising reasoning that would potentially be equally as made up?

The Gospel of Luke

The Gospel of Luke was written perhaps around 80-90 CE (although some conservative scholars favour an earlier date), or perhaps later, possibly by a Gentile companion of Paul. This, however, is contested by many scholars who think that the letters of Paul contradict the Gospel of Luke meaning that the author may not have known Paul. Some claim Luke is an anonymous or unknown author. Either way, it is generally accepted that Luke also wrote Acts. The early church fathers believed that the Gospel was written by Luke (a travelling physician), hence the name of the Gospel being attributed to him. As Theissen (1998, p.24) says, this view is only "occasionally put forward these days". There are, though, many contrasting opinions from every side of every fence, and huge works have been dedicated to what I am summing up in a paragraph or two.

By Luke's (and I will name the author so as to avoid confusion, cognisant of the point that this was probably not his name) own admission, he was trying to create some sort of a history. As the preface to Luke (1:1-3) sets out:

> Inasmuch as many have undertaken to compile an account of the things accomplished among us, just as they were handed down to us by those who from the beginning were eyewitnesses and servants of the word, it seemed fitting for me as well, having investigated everything carefully from the beginning, to write it out for you in consecutive order, most excellent Theophilus; so that you may know the exact truth about the things you have been taught.

This admits the author to being a non-eyewitness and sets his stall out. Many Christians claim that Luke is an excellent historian. However, as I mentioned earlier, Luke does not use a wide range of historiographical techniques that one would hope for from a good historian. Luke does, though, mention places and events with some degree of accuracy but I refer you to the Sherlock Holmes analogy. We know that even the very best ancient historians made mistakes and reported falsities. As Richard Carrier (who holds a PhD in ancient history) writes in *Not the Impossible Faith* (2009, p. 162):

> It is a universal principle accepted throughout the professional community that no ancient work is infallible. Even the most respected and trusted of historians — Thucydides, Polybius, Arrian — are believed to have reported some false information, especially when it came to private matters witnessed by only a few, and when material was important to an author's personal or dogmatic biases and presuppositions. And the further any ancient author is from these men in explicit methodology, by that much less are they trusted.

This is really important because it shows that, even with the best will in the world, Luke's Gospel will have at least a good sum of mistakes or false information. Some might say that this is easy to determine when the accounts disagree directly with the letters of Paul himself. And yet, it becomes very difficult to know otherwise, with any certainty, what is definitely true and what might be false at times when there is nothing to compare accounts to; no contradicting information. As Carrier continues (2009, p. 163):

> But on top of that we know he lied. For instance, his account of Paul's mission and the division it created in the Church contradicts Paul's own account (in his letter to the Galatians) in almost every single detail, and in a way we can discern was deliberate. And if Luke lied about that, he could be lying about anything else. Moreover, Luke cannot be classed with the best historians of his day because he never engages discussions of sources and methods, whereas they did — and that is a major reason why modern historians hold such men as Thucydides and Polybius and Arrian in high esteem: they often discuss where they got their information, how they got their information, and what they did with it. It is their open and candid awareness of the problems posed by writing a critical history that marks them as especially competent. Even lesser historians (like Xenophon, Plutarch, or Suetonius) occasionally mention or

discuss their sources, or acknowledge the existence of con-flicting accounts, and yet Luke doesn't even do that.

So that leaves us thinking that Luke, though he is probably more reliable than the other Gospel writers, is not a pillar of recti-tude by any stretch.

In addition, Luke probably used the Gospel of Mark and Q, as mentioned, as sources. His theology looks to designate "Jesus the Saviour anointed with the Spirit of God, who accepts the weak and outcast in the name of God and proclaims salvation to them."[1] As seen, the idea of Q could be wide of the mark, leading to prob-ability that Luke stole off Matthew. However, it potentially gets worse for Luke since there are some well-founded theories which posit that Luke plagiarised Jewish historian Josephus in much of his writing in Luke-Acts. Academics such as Josephan scholar Steve Mason and Richard Carrier favour such a conclusion. As Carrier notes in *Luke and Josephus* (2000):

> This thesis, if correct, entails two things. First, it un-dermines the historicity of certain details in the Christ story unique to Luke, such as his account of the Nativity, since these have been drawn from Josephus, who does not men-tion them in connection with Jesus, and thus it is more than possible that they never were linked with Jesus until Luke decided they were. This does not prove, but provides sup-port for the view that Luke is creating history, not recording it. Second, it settles the *terminus post quem* of the date Luke-Acts was written: for in order to draw material from the Jewish War, Luke could not have written before 79 A.D., and could well have written much later since the rate of publication in antiquity was exceedingly limited and slow, requiring hand copies made by personal slaves (though at first oral recitations would be more common than written copies); and in order to draw material from the Jewish Antiquities, as he appears to have done, Luke could not have written before 94 A.D., and again could have written much later for the same reason.

---

[1] Theissen (1998, p.32)

17

This fits better with the claims that the story has been "handed down to us" (1:2). It is also pertinent to note that Luke claims that "many" others have set out to write Gospels (1:1) but that his, with an air of special pleading, is the real deal!

So, finally, with all of this in mind, let us look at what Luke says about the birth of Jesus. Luke gives a genealogical account of Jesus, tracing the lineage right back to Adam. Mary is visited and forewarned, and Zacharias has a prophecy. Mary and Joseph travel to Bethlehem from Nazareth for a census where Jesus is laid down and angels proclaim his arrival to some shepherds who come to praise him. Forty days later he is presented at the Temple in Jerusalem, whereupon they return to Nazareth. I have omitted verses 21-38, the Presentation at the Temple, as it is not so important for the purposes of this book:

Jesus' Birth in Bethlehem

1 Now in those days a decree went out from Caesar Augustus, that a census be taken of all the inhabited earth. 2 This was the first census taken while Quirinius was governor of Syria. 3 And everyone was on his way to register for the census, each to his own city. 4 Joseph also went up from Galilee, from the city of Nazareth, to Judea, to the city of David which is called Bethlehem, because he was of the house and family of David, 5 in order to register along with Mary, who was engaged to him, and was with child. 6 While they were there, the days were completed for her to give birth. 7 And she gave birth to her firstborn son; and she wrapped Him in cloths, and laid Him in a manger, because there was no room for them in the inn.

8 In the same region there were *some* shepherds staying out in the fields and keeping watch over their flock by night. 9 And an angel of the Lord suddenly stood before them, and the glory of the Lord shone around them; and they were terribly frightened. 10 But the angel said to them, "Do not be afraid; for behold, I bring you good news of great joy which will be for all the people; 11 for today in the city of David there has been born for you a Savior, who is Christ the Lord. 12 This *will be* a sign for you: you will find a baby wrapped in cloths and lying in a manger." 13 And

suddenly there appeared with the angel a multitude of the heavenly host praising God and saying,

¹⁴ "Glory to God in the highest, And on earth peace among men with whom He is pleased."

¹⁵ When the angels had gone away from them into heaven, the shepherds *began* saying to one another, "Let us go straight to Bethlehem then, and see this thing that has happened which the Lord has made known to us." ¹⁶ So they came in a hurry and found their way to Mary and Joseph, and the baby as He lay in the manger. ¹⁷ When they had seen this, they made known the statement which had been told them about this Child. ¹⁸ And all who heard it wondered at the things which were told them by the shepherds. ¹⁹ But Mary treasured all these things, pondering them in her heart. ²⁰ The shepherds went back, glorifying and praising God for all that they had heard and seen, just as had been told them.

...

Return to Nazareth

³⁹ When they had performed everything according to the Law of the Lord, they returned to Galilee, to their own city of Nazareth. ⁴⁰ The Child continued to grow and become strong, increasing in wisdom; and the grace of God was upon Him.

This should serve as reference for the rest of the book as this is the core infancy account given in Luke. Although I will refer to Luke's genealogy, it is not necessary to reproduce it here.

Luke also gives an account, which I have not referenced here, of the birth of John the Baptist. What is interesting here is that the foretelling (1:5-25) is longer than that of Jesus (1:26-38). Luke, in recounting the Magnificat ("The Song of Mary") (1:46-56) where Mary exalts the Lord, is clearly referencing the "Song of Hannah" of the Old Testament (1 Samuel 2:1-11). They are strikingly similar—it is clear that Luke is reinterpreting The Song of Hannah and using it within his own theological framework. What is fascinating here is that the song of Hannah refers to someone who is too old to give birth. This is the situation of John the Baptist's mother Elizabeth, not Mary. Thus one can argue, and scholars such as Robert Price have, that this extract (The Magnificat) actually belonged to the John the Baptist narrative, originally, and was co-opted by Luke in its application to Jesus. This then casts doubt on these accounts of Mary, with regard to the forthcoming birth, since they were originally accounts of Elizabeth and John the Baptist's forthcoming birth. Unfortunately, the scriptures originally belonging to the John the Baptist cult no longer survive. However, there is reference to their arguments within the New Testament itself, as well as other early writing. As David Fitzgerald states, in *Nailed: Ten Myths That Show Jesus Never Existed At All* (2010, p. 153-154):

> Surprisingly, John the Baptist's sect was another rival competing with early Christianity. The 2nd century *Clementine Recognitions* even preserves their arguments against the Christians, and traces of the conflict are still in the New Testament: Luke 3:15 tries to downplay the fact that some argued that John was Christ. In several verses (Matthew 9:14, Mark 2:18 and Luke 5:33), the disciples of John the Baptist actually confront and argue with Jesus himself.
>
> Luke's Gospel begins with what was clearly originally scripture from the Baptist cult. Among other textual indications, John the Baptist's nativity story is four times longer than Jesus' in Luke, it takes very little editing to completely separate out the elements involving Jesus and Mary from John's nativity story, and the story doesn't suffer at all from

So to conclude, how can we summarise the Gospel of Luke, in general terms? Although Luke is more reliable than the other Gospel writers, we cannot be sure of his reliability (and we know there will be *at least some* inaccuracies), and we do not know the sources he uses (other than guessing at the Gospel of Mark and Q or Josephus). He obviously has a pro-Jesus bias and was not an eyewitness of Jesus' ministry. Furthermore, he would have had a slim chance of accessing primary evidence of Jesus' birth. He also seems to have used accounts of other people and stolen them in applying them to Jesus, casting doubt on whether they happened in the context of Jesus at all.

The Gospel of Matthew

As with the other Gospels, there are differing views as to the date, sources and composition of the Gospel of Matthew. One has to be careful because presuppositions over either the truth or the falsity of biblical narratives lead scholars to favour early or late dating (or compositional conclusions) accordingly. This is why I have favoured the work of Theissen who gives an overview of most of the relevant research, getting as close to an objective conclusion as possible.

Matthew's Gospel was written by an anonymous author sometime towards the end of the 1st century CE, probably being written in Syria.[1] Again, like Luke, it seems to be based on Mark and Q. Matthew contains almost the whole of the Gospel of Mark in one form or another, the birth narrative, though, being a clear addition.

The author was probably a highly educated Jew. This is because he corrects some fairly basic mistakes which Mark made about Judaism that any Jew would not have done. These include such things as misquoting the 10 commandments, as well as attributing God's words to Moses, and having Jews buy things on the Sabbath (something which was forbidden). He also showed intimate knowledge of Jewish law.

It is thought that Matthew references the destruction of the Temple in Jerusalem which happened in 70 CE, so it must have been composed later than that.

Matthew's theology is one that reflects Jesus' dignity, showing his life to fulfil the Law and Prophets, and presents him as a teacher who "unfolds the will of God".[2] It is accepted that he was writing for a Jewish audience.[3] Matthew seems to use the miracles of Jesus in a different way to his source, Mark, showing the more divine nature of Jesus.

---

[1] It refers (19:1) to Judea being *beyond* Jordan, thus implying the writer is not in Judea, as well as giving other hints.

[2] Theissen (1998, p.31)

[3] As per Delbert Burkett in *An Introduction To The New Testament And The Origins Of Christianity*

Now let us turn to the infancy narratives. The Gospel of Matthew gives us a different account of events to the Gospel of Luke, detailing separate events altogether, in some cases. An important piece of information is that the first two chapters of Matthew and the first three of Luke may not have been in the original manuscripts, but interpolated by later writers (we only have extant copies of the Gospels from much later centuries). As Martin A. Larson says in the book *The Essene-Christian Faith* (1989, p. 175):

> The first two chapters of Matthew and the first three chapters of Luke were added in the second century by Hellenizers who would accept only a divinely born 'savior-G-d' like those of the pagan mystery-cults.[1]

Matthew starts with a genealogy which reflects the first words of the Old Testament in the words used. Instead of Adam as the starting ancestor, the lineage is traced back to Abraham, the father of Judaism. An angel appears to Joseph to alert him that Mary's child was as a result of the Holy Spirit and not someone else (Matthew 1:18-25):

> [18] Now the birth of Jesus Christ was as follows: when His mother Mary had been betrothed to Joseph, before they came together she was found to be with child by the Holy Spirit. [19] And Joseph her husband, being a righteous man and not wanting to disgrace her, planned to send her away secretly. [20] But when he had considered this, behold, an angel of the Lord appeared to him in a dream, saying, "Joseph, son of David, do not be afraid to take Mary as your wife; for the Child who has been conceived in her is of the Holy Spirit. [21] She will bear a Son; and you shall call His name Jesus, for He will save His people from their sins." [22] Now all this took place to fulfil what was spoken by the Lord through the prophet: [23] "BEHOLD, THE VIR-

---

[1] Dr James Tabor also concludes, when talking of the manuscripts used by some of the earliest Christians (Ebionites), "Whatever Hebrew Matthew they used, did not contain chapters 1-2. This information is found in the writings of Jerome and Epiphanius."

GIN SHALL BE WITH CHILD AND SHALL BEAR A SON, AND THEY SHALL CALL HIS NAME IMMANUEL," which translated means, "GOD WITH US." ²⁴ And Joseph awoke from his sleep and did as the angel of the Lord commanded him, and took *Mary* as his wife, ²⁵ but kept her a virgin until she gave birth to a Son; and he called His name Jesus.

Before I go on, it is certainly worth noting that the importance with which Matthew imbues the title "Immanuel" seems wholly misplaced since, though he makes big claims of Jesus having fulfilled this Old Testament prophecy, the title is not used anywhere else in the New Testament, let alone with regard to Jesus. Apologists might claim that this is a reinterpretation of the Old Testament writing, but this simply raises further questions. Furthermore, there is one major difference between the narrative here and Luke in that Matthew has them living in Bethlehem already:

The Visit of the Magi

¹ Now after Jesus was born in Bethlehem of Judea in the days of Herod the king, magi from the east arrived in Jerusalem, saying, ² "Where is He who has been born King of the Jews? For we saw His star in the east and have come to worship Him." ³ When Herod the king heard *this*, he was troubled, and all Jerusalem with him. ⁴ Gathering together all the chief priests and scribes of the people, he inquired of them where the Messiah was to be born. ⁵ They said to him, "In Bethlehem of Judea; for this is what has been written by the prophet:

⁶ 'AND YOU, BETHLEHEM, LAND OF JUDAH, ARE BY NO MEANS LEAST AMONG THE LEADERS OF JUDAH; FOR OUT OF YOU SHALL COME FORTH A RULER WHO WILL SHEPHERD MY PEOPLE ISRAEL.'"

⁷ Then Herod secretly called the magi and determined from them the exact time the star appeared.⁸ And he sent them to Bethlehem and said, "Go and search carefully for the Child; and when you have found *Him*, report to me, so that I too may come and worship Him." ⁹ After hearing the king, they went their way; and the star, which they had

seen in the east, went on before them until it came and stood over *the place* where the Child was. [10] When they saw the star, they rejoiced exceedingly with great joy. [11] After coming into the house they saw the Child with Mary His mother; and they fell to the ground and worshiped Him. Then, opening their treasures, they presented to Him gifts of gold, frankincense, and myrrh. [12] And having been warned *by God* in a dream not to return to Herod, the magi left for their own country by another way.

We have reference to Herod, as opposed to the census, and we have magi visiting Jesus, and not shepherds. Next, we have Jesus' family fleeing immediately to Egypt (no Temple presentation) and Herod massacring children in the search for this newborn 'usurper':

The Flight to Egypt

[13] Now when they had gone, behold, an angel of the Lord *appeared to Joseph in a dream and said, "Get up! Take the Child and His mother and flee to Egypt, and remain there until I tell you; for Herod is going to search for the Child to destroy Him."

[14] So Joseph got up and took the Child and His mother while it was still night, and left for Egypt. [15]He remained there until the death of Herod. *This was* to fulfil what had been spoken by the Lord through the prophet: "OUT OF EGYPT I CALLED MY SON."

Herod Slaughters Babies

[16] Then when Herod saw that he had been tricked by the magi, he became very enraged, and sent and slew all the male children who were in Bethlehem and all its vicinity, from two years old and under, according to the time which he had determined from the magi. [17] Then what had been spoken through Jeremiah the prophet was fulfilled:

[18] "A VOICE WAS HEARD IN RAMAH, WEEPING AND GREAT MOURNING, RACHEL WEEPING FOR HER CHILDREN; AND SHE REFUSED TO BE COMFORTED, BECAUSE THEY WERE NO MORE."

¹⁹ But when Herod died, behold, an angel of the Lord *appeared in a dream to Joseph in Egypt, and said, ²⁰ "Get up, take the Child and His mother, nd go into the land of Israel; for those who sought the Child's life are dead." ²¹ So Joseph got up, took the Child and His mother, and came into the land of Israel. ²² But when he heard that Archelaus was reigning over Judea in place of his father Herod, he was afraid to go there. Then after being warned *by God* in a dream, he left for the regions of Galilee, ²³ and came and lived in a city called Nazareth. *This was* to fulfil what was spoken through the prophets: "He shall be called a Nazarene."

We then have Jesus' family *moving* to Nazareth, in order to 'fulfil' a prophecy that the Messiah will be a Nazarene. More analysis will elucidate this further later in the book.

It seems that Matthew recounts a good many things which seem incredible in their omission from every other source. As Brown (1977, p. 36):

Matthew's accounts contains a number of extraordinary or miraculous public events that, were they factual, should have left some traces in Jewish records or elsewhere in the NT (the king and all Jerusalem upset over the birth of the Messiah in Bethlehem; a star which moved from Jerusalem south to Bethlehem and came to rest over a house; the massacre of all the male children in Bethlehem).

In conclusion, Matthew's Gospel is again anonymous, written by an educated Jew in the 80s or 90s CE who was a non-eyewitness to Jesus' ministries and who was also a pro-Jesus evangelist. There are even fewer historiographical techniques in this Gospel than in Luke, and so we can possibly assume a larger degree of inaccuracy.

Hopefully, both in this section and the section on the Gospel of Luke, enough of the biblical text is articulated here in order for it to act as an easier reference guide than having a Bible open next to you.

I will now endeavour to set out the issues with these biblical narratives, both in conjunction and independently, that I and

25

many others have which should draw the reader to conclude that they did not occur (certainly in the manner in which they are portrayed in the Bible).

PART 2 – PRE-CENSUS ARGU-MENTS AGAINST THE HISTORICITY OF THE NATIVITY ACCOUNTS

---

1 - The Virgin Birth

I will try and approach things in a vaguely chronological or-der and since births require conceptions, and this is really about conception, the virgin birth seems as good a place as any to start the ball rolling.

The notion that Jesus was born of a virgin is a contentious issue because there is much mythological precedent for such a birth. For people who believe that the entire persona of Jesus is fictional (who believe in the 'Jesus myth'), a virgin birth fits in very well with the notion that the infancy narratives are mytho-logical.

We essentially have the Holy Spirit impregnating Mary, who was a virgin at the time, although as Raymond E. Brown says in *The Birth of the Messiah* (1977, p. 124-5), the Holy Spirit is read as being a creative influence as opposed to anything sexual. As the angel Gabriel told her in Luke 1:35: "The Holy Spirit will come upon you, and the power of the Most High will overshadow you; and for that reason the holy Child shall be called the Son of God." It is fairly explicitly explained that the Holy Spirit will be responsible for the conception, and true to the angelic words, Mary fell pregnant with a God for a son. Some sceptics claim that Luke does not deny the possibility that Mary could not have got pregnant naturally between the Annunciation and the conception.

On the other hand, some liberal commentators suggest that the virgin birth claim was an answer to counter-claims that Mary

27

conceived illegitimately. In order to cover up this rather embarrassing situation, a virgin birth is supposed. I would probably side with Christian apologists who state that this is a highly unlikely excuse. In reality, if my partner got pregnant without my assistance, and the neighbours heard that this was the case only to be told "actually, it's the Son of God, impregnated immaculately by the Holy Spirit", then one would be met with ridicule. Also, the claim that Jesus was actually illegitimate and this was simply a defensive ruse cannot run alongside other claims that are also thrown about. For example, as we shall see, some claim that the word for virgin is a mistranslation. It cannot both be a mistranslation *and* a defensive ruse. Such sceptics cannot have it both ways.[1]

James Tabor, in *The Jesus Dynasty: The Hidden History of Jesus, His Royal Family, and the Birth of Christianity* (2007, p. 64-72), claims that, due to similar accusations of Roman philosopher Celsus, Jesus' father was actually Panthera (or Pantera or Pandera), a Roman soldier serving in the area at the time of Jesus' conception. While this holds with some more fringe scholars, the theory is generally rejected by most mainstream scholars. Interestingly though, if we take (as we shall see in the next section) the word *almah*, used to describe Mary, as meaning a nubile young woman, and not virgin, and we see it in context of Matthew's genealogy of Jesus, then perhaps Tabor is not far off. Tamar, Rahab, Ruth and Bathsheba are women bizarrely included in a patrilineal genealogy (as we shall also see) and were all known adulterers and harlots. With Mary included as a female in this list, perhaps Matthew is hinting something covertly.

However, not all of the early Christians accepted a claim of virgin birth[2], seeing it as a pagan influence on their religion. Justin Martyr (in about 135 CE), for example, conceded this much in his *Dialogue with the Trypho*. He claims that most Christians did not believe the virgin birth claim, but he *did* believe it, not on evidence, but on prophecy:

---

[1] As Charles Foster states in *The Christmas Mystery* (2007, p.80).

[2] And as Brown (1977, p. 301-303) suggests, there are some modern scholars who debate whether Luke originally claimed a virginal conception or whether this was added as an afterthought, either by someone else, or by Luke himself. He sees these claims as being not quite persuasive enough.

It is quite true that some people of our kind acknowledge him to be Christ, but at the same time declare him to have been a man of men. I, however, cannot agree with them, and will not do so, even if the majority [of Christians] insist on this opinion and impart it to me ; for by Christ ourself we have been commanded to base our conclusions, not on human teachings, but on predictions set forth by the blessed prophets and imparted in his own teaching.[1]

So the virgin birth claim was even a little controversial to the contemporary Christian church[2]. Let us put Jesus' birth into comparative context. Patrick Campbell in *The Mythical Jesus* (1965, p. 45) points out that Hercules, Osiris, Bacchus, Mithra,

---

[1] Fred Cornwallis Conybeare in *Myths, Magic and Morals*, 1910, p.180

[2] There is much controversy too as to whether the Christian movement borrowed from Mithraism. I do not want to enter into this long-standing debate in this book since one could write a book merely on the arguments of comparative similarities between Christianity and its sister religion Mithraism alone. It is an interesting area, no doubt, and worth further reading. Suffice to say, As Kerry Temple in an article in The Humanist points out (Who Do Men Say That I Am?, The Humanist, May/June 1991, p. 4.):

[Mithras] was said to have been sent by a father-god to vanquish darkness and evil in the world. Born of a virgin (a birth witnessed only by shepherds), Mithras was described variously as the Way, the Truth, the Light, the Word, the Son of God, and the Good Shepherd and was often depicted carrying a lamb upon his shoulders. Followers of Mithras celebrated December 25th (the winter solstice) by ringing bells, singing hymns, lighting candles, giving gifts, and administering a sacrament of bread and water. Between December 25th and the spring equinox (Easter, from the Latin for earth goddess) came the 40 days' search for Osiris, a god of justice and love. The cult also observed Black Friday, commemorating Mithras' sacrificial bull-slaying which fructified the earth. Worn out by the battle, Mithras is symbolically represented as a corpse and is placed in a sacred rock tomb from which he is removed after three days in a festival of rejoicing.

29

Hermes, Prometheus, Perseus and Horus share some intriguing characteristics with Jesus, as all were thought to have[1]:

- Been male.
- Lived in pre-Christian times.
- Had a god for a father.
- Had a human virgin for a mother.
- Had their birth announced by a heavenly display.
- Had their birth announced by celestial music.
- Been born about Dec 25th.
- had an attempt on their life by a tyrant while they were still an infant
- Met with a violent death.
- Rose again from the dead.

Almost all were believed to have:

- Been visited by "wise men" during infancy.
- Fasted for 40 days as an adult.

There is certainly a suspicious similarity between these stories, all of which predate the Christian version. So why the reliance on virgin births in these great stories? Miraculous births, whether virgin or otherwise, are commonplace motifs in ancient literature and culture since such an event clearly signposts a very important being coming into the world. These births break natural laws and appear impossibly wonderful, and they act as a herald welcoming the figure into earthly existence. From a cynical point of view, in order to compete with all of these other religions and myths, which were themselves believed to varying degrees, and in order for Jesus to be taken seriously, a miraculous birth is simply a prerequisite.

Even Julius Caesar is claimed to have been descended from Aeneas, supposed son of the goddess Venus. More importantly was the birth of Emperor Caesar Augustus. He was claimed to have born of the god Apollo. As liberal theologian John Dominic Crossan, in *The Birth of Christianity*, states (1999, p. 287-29):

---

[1] As referenced at http://www.religioustolerance.org/virgin_b1.htm (retrieved 07/01/2012)

30

Augustus came from a miraculous conception by the divine and human conjunction of [the God] Apollo and [his mother] Atia. How does the historian respond to that story? Are there any who take it literally? ... That divergence raises an ethical problem for me. Either all such divine conceptions, from Alexander to Augustus and from the Christ to the Buddha, should be accepted literally and miraculously or all of them should be accepted metaphorically and theologically. It is not morally acceptable to say ... our story is truth but yours is myth; ours is history but yours is a lie. It is even less morally acceptable to say that indirectly and covertly by manufacturing defensive or protective strategies that apply only to one's own story.

This is a crucially important point and it perfectly illustrates the use of the fallacy of special pleading employed by many Christian theologians and historians. Caesar Augustus is especially important because he was Emperor at the time of Jesus' birth and who, at the time, would have been enemy number one in Judea and surrounding areas. If Jesus was going to compete with anyone, it would make most sense to do so against the ruling God-like Emperor and subjugator of Jewish lands. Augustus called himself "Divi filius" (son of the Divine One) and "Dei filius" (Son of God) which, as scholars like Crossan have argued, might well have been co-opted by the Christians for Jesus.

Further to these claims from a comparative and hence external point of view, let us look briefly at whether there is any internal support for a virgin birth from the Bible itself. We can see a belief is certainly evident in Matthew and Luke, that much is seemingly obvious. The biblical writers who were active before this time were Paul and Mark. The Gospel of Mark has no infancy narrative, and we know that Luke and Matthew (particularly Matthew) used Mark as a source. Thus it appears that the infancy narratives are later additions. Surely if Mark had known about these miraculous accounts, and believed them, he would have included them? This appears somewhat suspect. This suspicion is increased when we look at the writing available from Paul, the earliest Christian writer, working around a couple of decades after the death of Jesus. There is no reference in any of Paul's remain-

31

ing writing, no allusion even, to a virgin birth. The event represents a conspicuous absence. Although Paul did not know Jesus personally, he did know James, the brother of Jesus (if a literal brother is implied in the text), and yet still reports no virginal mother of Jesus. Moreover, he implies a normal birth in some of his writings as he states that Jesus was "born of a woman" (Galatians 4:4) and was "descended from David, according to the flesh" (Romans 1:3).

The Old Testament sets some precedent for a miraculous birth in accounting for some strange births which were heralded by an angelic appearance to scared parents. Manoah was visited by an angel who told her, as with Mary, that she would give birth to a son who would be a Nazirite. This boy, heralded by an angel, was to be Samson. Obvious parallels, with the word Nazirite being a confusion (more on this later), can be drawn here. Samuel was born of Hannah who had had her womb "closed", and in praying to God, with Eli present, her prayers were answered (as mentioned before there are similarities to John the Baptist here) and she fell pregnant. A similar situation occurred with Isaac being born of Sarah.

The Gospel of John also implies a normal birth. The writer of John would have known about the virgin birth claims as the circulation of Matthew and Luke would most probably have lead to the writer knowing the Gospels as he wrote possibly as much as 15 or so years later. John 1:45 claims Jesus as "the son of Joseph" and John 6:42 states "Is not this Jesus, the son of Joseph, whose father and mother we know?" Further to this, the Gospel of Thomas, a non-canonical Gospel, gives no indication either that there was a virgin birth, as well as there being no mention in what has been thought to be Q (from various textual analyses of Matthew and Luke).

Therefore, it seems rather apparent (to the sceptic at least) that Jesus' birth of a virgin is not evidenced in the Bible itself. Some scholars indicate that Luke's early chapters are a later interpolation leaving the very real possibility that Matthew is the only independent source for the virgin birth account. Is it, then, good enough evidence to support such a massive claim? A mere collection of sentences with unknown sources staking such an improbable claim seems to make fairly heavy demands on our rationality in order to be believed.

In order to believe that Jesus was born of a virgin, there is a temptation to fall into the fallacy of special pleading. This is because one has to discount all other claims of miraculous births in order to settle on the one true miraculous birth. However, if one believes in the sort of creator God of the Christian variety, then this God can intervene and can do pretty much anything he wants. With this worldview comes an acceptance, implicit or explicit, of the supernatural. The naturalist will, *a priori*, usually deny the ability for supernatural events to occur. However, I want to try to judge these events from the point of view of a Christian. If you are Christian, then the sort of God you can believe in is the sort of God that can organise a virgin birth. It is a stretch for people who are naturalists, admittedly, and most supernaturalists would probably deny it for anyone other than their God. Therefore, it is not so much about whether it is logically possible, but whether it is evidentially probable. Of course, the supernatural claims are broad and many in the infancy narratives, most of which I will go into in further detail. Before the birth, depending on which Gospel you read, both Joseph and Mary and even Mary's relatives were visited by angels to be forewarned of what would happen. Angelic appearances have happened, albeit infrequently, throughout history in various cultures. What we need to decide here is whether the evidence provided is enough to convince us as to whether the biblical claims are true.

Aside from the ability for this to happen, I suppose one could say that it is not surprising, given that a god would be born, that said god would have quite some birth! Yet it is also worth noting the account of Luke 2:43-50, in which a twelve year-old Jesus becomes lost for three days. When his parents finally find him in the Temple, Mary says to Jesus:

> "Behold your father and I have been anxiously looking for you." Jesus replies "Why is it that you were looking for Me? Did you not know that I had to be in My Father's house?" But they did not understand the statement which He had made to them.

If Mary and Joseph knew that Jesus was conceived by the seed of God, and that God was indeed the Father, then it becomes a little baffling that they did not understand what Jesus was talking about. Again, this adds to the overall confusion and doubt over the veracity of the miraculous birth claim.

One could claim that this story, only to be found in Luke, might have been taken from the Infancy Gospels such as the Infancy Gospel of Thomas, a fanciful account of the childhood of Jesus containing many miraculous claims. Of course, if this one childhood story was borrowed from Thomas, then the date for Luke is pushed even further back. Food for thought, at any rate.[1]

Thus given the comparative accounts of miraculous births, and given the Roman context of Jesus' birth, it does become somewhat suspect as a claim. As part of a cumulative case, the implausibility of a virgin birth has a good deal of weight. It is a widely critiqued supposition of Christianity, especially from the Jesus myth camp. The event of a miraculous birth for Jesus is sometimes seen as necessary for establishing his divinity and if such an event is cast into doubt, then perhaps so too is his divinity.

---

[1] Scholar Robert M. Price discusses this relation to the Infancy Gospels in *Incredible Shrinking Son Of Man: How Reliable I s The Gospel Tradition?*

2 - The mistranslation of virgin

One of the most commonly referenced issues regarding the infancy narratives revolves around a simple word and its translation. Before I explain this, let me give a little history lesson as to how the Hebrew Bible was put together. The Jewish religion had the Tanakh which was a collection of books in Hebrew which broadly covered the Christian Old Testament. The Greek empire stretched over Judea and surrounding areas as a result of Alexander the Great's exploits. This was known as the Selucid Empire. In order to allow the Tanakh to be accessed by those many Greek speaking Jews that were around, it was decided to have it translated into Koine Greek. This version is called the Septuagint, which means "translation of the seventy", due to the legend in which seventy-two elders were supposedly put into seventy-two separate rooms only to come up with seventy-two identical translations (with God's help).

Thus the original Hebrew books were translated into Greek anywhere from the 3rd Century BCE to as late as 132 BCE. Isaiah 7:14 uses a particular word, *almah*, whose meaning is variously "young woman", "girl" or "virgin". Jewish and secular scholars have argued that it is this word which has caused much trouble in the interpretation of the prophecy of Isaiah 7:

> Therefore the Lord Himself will give you a sign: Behold, a virgin will be with child and bear a son, and she will call His name Immanuel. He will eat curds and honey at the time He knows *enough* to refuse evil and choose good. For before the boy will know *enough* to refuse evil and choose good, the land whose two kings you dread will be forsaken. (7:14-16)

This is one of the most referenced prophecies predicting Jesus as Messiah, and why Jesus was (in a manner of self-fulfilling prophecy?) named Immanuel. Aside from the fact that the rest of the prophecy makes no sense with its issues of good and evil, we have the key verse which talks of a virgin bearing a child.

35

This translation used by Matthew, according to sceptics, is erroneous. This translation made by Matthew is incorrect it is claimed, since the original Hebrew word *almah* means young woman in the same way that *elem*, the equivalent, simply means young man. Matthew uses the Greek word *parthenos* which exclusively means virgin. The more proper Hebrew word for virgin is *bethulah*, it is similarly claimed. As such, it is possible that because Matthew uses a mistranslation of an original Messianic prophecy, he mistakenly thought that the Messiah *had* to be born of a virgin rather than simply a young woman.

The standard Christian defence of this is that in other instances where *almah* is used to refer to a young girl, the person has on occasion at least incidentally been a virgin. Moreover, they claim that *bethulah* itself can sometimes refer to women who are *not* virgins (such as Esther 2:8-17) and is sometimes used with a phrase to clarify that the woman has not known a man. However, for critics, the use of *almah* in Isaiah would suggest a correct translation would be young woman as opposed to virgin since it appears to refer to a wife of King Ahaz. Importantly for the translation of the Hebrew word *almah*, the Aramaic and Ugaritic cognate terms are both used of women who are not virgins, more commonly in the context of age.[1] One problem Christians face is that if "virgin" is the translation it has a definite article ("the") rather than an indefinite article ("a") required by "a virgin"[2]

---

[1] It is really worth checking out the lexical information about the Isaiah passage as set out in the NET Notes in the NET Bible: http://classic.net.bible.org/verse.php?book=Isa&chapter=7&verse=14 (retrieved 10/03/2012). For example, "In Isa 7:14 one could translate, "the young woman is pregnant." In this case the woman is probably a member of the royal family. Another option, the one followed in the present translation, takes the adjective in an imminent future sense, "the young woman is about to conceive." In this case the woman could be a member of the royal family, or, more likely, the prophetess with whom Isaiah has sexual relations shortly after this."

[2] There was an excellent linguistic resource online about the Isaiah passage and use of *almah* on the www.messiahtruth.com website (http://www.messiahtruth.com/is714a.html). However, at the time of publishing the website was not available, though the document can be found variously online (search for Messiah Truth and Isaiah 7:14). This

meaning that a reference to an unknown woman in the future is less likely.

One strong piece of evidence in favour of the apologists is the fact that the translators of the Tanakh into Greek originally translated it so. Yet this merely focuses the problem one step further back. Charles Isbell, in his 1977 article "Does the Gospel of Matthew Proclaim Mary's Virginity?" in *Biblical Archaeological Review*, claims that the debate is somewhat moot since no Hebrew word really does justice to the concept of virginity. Charles Foster, on the other hand, in *The Christmas Mystery*, (2007) suggests something different by claiming that even if the original prophecies do not refer to a virgin birth then it is even more likely that the virgin claim is true since it is irrespective of the Old Testament. He concludes (p. 84-5):

> The notion of the virginal conception of Jesus was not only theologically unnecessary but ... positively harmful. The church, quite frankly, would have been better off without it. Its origins cannot be traced to Judaism, and although there are some analogies between Jesus' birth and the birth of some god-spawned heroes in the ancient world, the analogies are not good enough to indicate that the pagan stories caused the Christian stories. Nobody would have read the Christian stories as asserting that the claims of Jesus trumped those classical heroes or the Roman Emperors.
>
> Of course, the virgin birth can't be proved. But where a claim has no precedent and no obvious benefit it is legitimate to wonder if it has been made because it is true.

I think that this conclusion is somewhat hopeful. Foster claims that, being harmful to the church, it would not have been claimed by Matthew. But how could Matthew have known that in the future it would have been harmful? Moreover, many argue that it *can* and *was* read in ways that acted to trump Roman mythological and Emperor claims since much of the early church was centred around Rome and the Roman Empire. The reason for

---

resource gives a complete and formidable deconstruction of the apologist claims that Isaiah 7 both contains reference to a virgin and to Jesus.

the early Christian flourishing *was* the Roman Empire and its gentile converts: the roads, the logistical ease with which both trade and ideas could pass around the Empire, and of course the Emperor Constantine a little later. As for there not being precedent, we have plenty of strange birth precedents in the Old Testament. More importantly, in the Greek and Roman influenced region there were plenty of comparative virgin births from Greek, Roman and other regional cultures. The Christian claim seems, to me at least, to fit *exceptionally well* into that paradigm, as we saw in the last section.

The debate is still strong, since many Bible translations use "young woman" as opposed to "virgin"[1]. What is perhaps more evident is the idea that Isaiah 7 doesn't refer to Jesus at all, but as Bishop John Shelby Spong says[2], it is more likely a prophecy that was fulfilled during the Syro-Ephraimite invasion of Judah and the siege of Jerusalem by the combined armies of the Northern Kingdom and Syria in around 735 BCE. The child born to the young woman was supposedly a sign that the Jerusalem siege would end and the city would continue to thrive as it did before the conflict. A reading of the whole passage in context leads one to conclude that this must be the case. It certainly seems like the prophecy has been forcefully co-opted, shoehorned even, into predicting Jesus as Messiah.

As such, it is almost irrelevant as to whether the prophecy refers to a young woman or a virgin since it is a prophecy which clearly does not refer to Jesus' birth. As biblical scholar and liberal Christian Thom Stark, in *The Human Faces of God: What Scripture Reveals When It Gets God Wrong (and Why Inerrancy Tries to Hide It)*, illustrates (2011, p. 28):

> ...the point is moot. Even if Isaiah *did* mean "virgin", he was not predicting a miraculous birth. If the woman had been a virgin at the time Isaiah uttered the prophecy, she would not have been by the time she had conceived the child. However, the verb here, "to conceive" (*harah*), is in

---

[1] For example, the Revised English Bible, the Revised Standard Version, James Moffatt Translation and the New Revised Standard Version.

[2] J.S. Spong, "A religious Santa Claus tale: The birth narrative of Jesus shouldn't be taken literally"

the perfect tense, which means it is a completed action. The best translation of the verse would reflect that the young woman was *already* pregnant, that Isaiah was predicting the child's *gender*, and directing her how to name him: "Look, this young pregnant woman is going to have a son, and she shall name him Emmanuel."

Stark continues to show how the Isaiah passage cannot possibly refer to Jesus, a considerable amount of time later, putting the verses into the context of the recent Assyrian conquest, and the child having to eat "cheese and honey" (uncultivated food) as opposed to bread and wine. Given that it quite obviously seems that this passage is a prophecy involving Ahaz and not Jesus, then it seems more likely that *almah* does actually refer to "young woman". In order to translate it as "virgin" one has to take the prophecy well out of context and use the word in its more unlikely form.

It has been claimed that this prophecy, then, was a dual prophecy predicting two different outcomes. However, dual prophecies have no precedent—there are simply no other examples of such a thing. Another issue is that if the word does mean "virgin" then it must mean virgin for both prophecies but the first prophecy does not refer to a virgin, rather the wife of King Ahaz. Moreover, how could the verses 7:15-16 apply to Jesus? That is a simply nonsensical idea. With these and many other issues, the dual prophecy theory collapses before it gets off the ground.

It is interesting to note that most Bible translations (apart from, for example, The Revised Standard Version) which include the New Testament translate *almah* in Isaiah as "virgin". However, translations of the Hebrew Bible which do not include the New Testament merely translate the word as "young woman". For Jewish translators, as mentioned earlier, *youth* is what is implied by the term and not *virginity*. As Messiah Truth, a Jewish source, claims, "Other more accurate vocabulary was available to Isaiah had he desired to specifically refer here to a virgin—the Hebrew term בְּתוּלָה (*betulah*) means **a virgin**."[1]

---

[1] See footnote on p. 37.

As such, I posit that the Septuagint translators *and* Matthew mistranslated the passage and Matthew misappropriated the passage from Isaiah for his own theological ends.

3 - The male genome

Carrying on from the last section, there is a natural progression of thought when one considers that Jesus was immaculately conceived. One must look at these events reported from within the historical context in which they supposedly took place. The understanding of how the whole biology of reproduction took place was woefully inadequate as an accurate representation of reality. The Greeks had done some thinking on the subject. The *preformationists* believed that the father was like the plough and the mother the field. This meant that the seed and all the 'genetic' material was delivered by the father with the mother merely providing the milieu in which the development took place.

Later, Aristotle, based on research into animals, and recognising that children could look like more distant relatives, moved the thinking on a little. He believed the mother provided the *material cause* whilst the father provided the *moving cause*.

In effect, however, contemporary physiological understanding was fairly limited. Thus a claim that Jesus, as a man, came from an immaculate conception raised few eyebrows of surprise (biologically speaking).

The problem is that we now know better. Christians claim that Jesus was fully man, which meant that he was fully comparable to your next man. Your next man is conceived when the genetic material of the father, carried in the sperm, comes together with the genetic material from the mother, in the egg (ovum). These two genomes combine to create a new genome, without one of which you simply cannot have a viable living organism with a complete genome. Strictly speaking, without the genetic blueprints of both parents fusing, you simply will not get the conception and birth of a 'man'.

With thanks to scientists like Darwin, Watson and Crick we understand the importance of heredity, and understand the units of heredity and how they are sequenced. Our genotype (genetic blueprint) informs our phenotype (set of traits: physical, emotional, personality and otherwise). It is hard to see how Jesus could have had a viable genotype and resulting phenotype.

41

The result of this is twofold. Either it makes the immaculate conception impossible and renders such a claim redundant or it means that the male genome was magically fused with Mary's egg (or indeed another supernatural egg implanted into Mary) to make a fully workable genetic sequence.

If we take the first option, then that leaves us with the idea that the virgin birth is even more likely to be fiction than we have already discussed. The second option, a sort of theistic 'get out of jail free card' doesn't make life all that easier for the theist. It implies that the genome came from God in some capacity. This invalidates the claim that Jesus was fully man, since he was clearly half-God. If God somehow managed to input purely 'human' male genetic matter, then this prompts the question as to what criteria were used for deciding such a genome.

We can already surmise that Jesus was pretty much a perfect example of a man, from the Christian point of view. In a realistic sense, it is impossible for a 'real' human being to be that perfect, surely. So how can it be, with a genome selected by God, that Jesus can be hailed as being fully man? Let me refer to Hebrews 2:17:

> Therefore, He had to be made like His brethren in all things, so that He might become a merciful and faithful high priest in things pertaining to God, to make propitiation for the sins of the people.

Aside from the difficulties with being both fully man and fully God, as is claimed, and the notions that Christians equivocate over the terms *man* or *God* or both, we can see that the lack of proper understanding of genetic biology means that an immaculate conception presents quite a headache.

42

4 – The contradictory genealogies

Both the Gospel of Luke and the Gospel of Matthew contain genealogies which look to trace Jesus' lineage back to important people. Jesus was claimed to be the Messiah. Either this was prophesied in the Old Testament, or the other side of the coin is that the Gospel writers created stories, or fit existing Jesus stories into Old Testament frameworks, that would 'fulfil' these prophecies.

The contrived fulfilment of prophecy does seem to be the most probable explanation for the genealogies existing at all, from a critical point of view. There are countless prophecies in the Old Testament, from the likes of Hebrews, Psalms, Isaiah, Jeremiah and Genesis, which stake claims that the Messiah will come from the Davidic line or from Abraham, or from Judah or the "seed of a woman". The genealogies 'prove' all of this, it would appear. To the more critical reader, again, it is hard to see how many of these prophecies could be applied to Jesus by way of fact that they are either not prophetic writing or clearly do not refer to Jesus in the Old Testament contexts.

Of course, if we discount Joseph as being Jesus' real father then both genealogies are futile attempts to link Jesus to anybody.

Luke's genealogy is a long list of names which goes back to Adam, the first man, supposedly (we will ignore the huge elephant in the room of human genetics, history, anthropology, palaeontology and so on). Luke does start with the important words "When He began His ministry, Jesus Himself was about thirty years of age, being, as was supposed, the son of Joseph..." This "supposed" seems to refer to the virgin birth scenario. Obviously this genealogy (as we understand heredity) does not *relate* Jesus to anybody since Joseph was not Jesus' biological father. This means that it could be read in a legalistic sense.

God	Terah	Eliakim	Joanan
Adam	Abraham	Jonam	Joda
Seth	Isaac	Joseph	Josech
Enosh	Jacob	Judah	Semein
Kenan	Judah	Simeon	Mattathias
Mahalalel	Pharez	Levi	Mahath
Jared	Hezron	Matthat	Naggai
Enoch	Ram	Jorim	Hesli
Methuselah	Amminadab	Eliezer	Nahum
Lamech	Nahshon	Joshua	Amos
Noah	Salmon	Er	Mattathias
Shem	Boaz	Elmadam	Joseph
Arphaxad	Obed	Cosam	Jannai
Cainan	Jesse	Addi	Melchi
Shelah	David	Melchi	Levi
Eber	Nathan	Neri	Matthat
Peleg	Mattatha	Shealtiel	Heli
Reu	Menna	Zerubbabel	(as was sup-
Serug	Melea	Rhesa	posed) Joseph
Nahor			Jesus

Luke's 77 generations used in the genealogy is a symbolic number representing, according to early theologian Augustine, the forgiveness of sin. Seven was a very important number for the time and so it looks like Luke might be counting in groups of seven. As mentioned, one of the crucial points of the genealogies was to link Jesus through to David so to prove that Jesus was of Davidic stock. This fulfils some vital prophecies which predict that the Messiah will come of the House of David[1], liberally scattered around the Old Testament. Something which I will return to later is the fact that Luke represents Jesus as being 42 generations after David, which is no small amount of time.

One issue for Luke is this quote from 1 Chronicles 22:9-10:

> But you will have a son who will be a man of peace and rest, and I will give him rest from all his enemies on every side. His name will be Solomon, and I will grant Is-

---

[1] For example, Psalms 89:3-4 Psalms 132:11, Isaiah 16:5, Jeremiah 23:5-6, Isaiah 11:1–10

rael peace and quiet during his reign. He is the one who
will build a house for my Name. He will be my son, and I
will be his father. And I will establish the throne of his
kingdom over Israel forever.'

This is problematic due to the prophecy that Jesus is not, in
Luke's genealogy at any rate, a descendent of Solomon, but of his
brother Nathan. This means that the Messianic prophecy of this
extract is not fulfilled in Jesus, which is potentially critical for
Luke's claims.

Abraham	Amminadab	Solomon	Jotham	Shealtiel	Eliud
Isaac	Nahshon	Rehoboam	Ahaz	Zerubbabel	Eleazar
Jacob	Salmon &	Abijam	Hezekiah	Abiud	Matthan
Judah &	Rahab	Asa	Manasseh	Eliakim	Jacob
Tamar	Boaz &	Jehosaphat	Amon	Azor	Joseph
Pharez	Ruth	Jehoram	Josiah	Zadok	& Mary
Hezron	Obed	Uzziah	Jeconiah	Achim	Jesus
Ram	Jesse				
	David &				
	Wife of				
	Uriah				

So what of the Gospel of Matthew? Matthew's genealogy is
somewhat different both in number of generations and in person-
nel. Numerology is just as important to Matthew, perhaps more
so. He sets the lineage out in three sets of fourteen, based on
landmark events in biblical history. Again, as with Luke, this
makes the genealogy rely on the factor of seven. The number
fourteen is the *gamatria* of David—the numerical value of his
name. These events are the formation of Israel, the Babylonian
captivity and Jesus as Messiah split into the respective groups as
can be seen in the previous table. As Matthew 1:17 says:

So all the generations from Abraham to David are
fourteen generations; from David to the deportation to
Babylon, fourteen generations; and from the deportation to
Babylon to the Messiah, fourteen generations.

There is a genealogy in 1 Chronicles 3 which overlaps Matthew's and it seems like he has omitted three names (Joash, Amaziah, and Azoriah) which undermines one of the two lists. This is probably Matthew's doing—it could well be an opportunity to lose a few names for numerical reasons, and these kings were particularly wicked, coming to infamous ends by God's will. Also, two Jeconiahs seem to have been melded into one. The fact that the genealogies differ from the Old Testament list is telling, though.

There are only thirteen names in the last tesseradecad (a group of fourteen names). This is not thought to be a simple mistake of miscounting on the part of Matthew and as a result many second guesses have been put forward. For example, Mary could be counted as a generation alongside Joseph; Jeconiah could be doubled as mentioned; names at the beginning or end of the tesseradecads after David could be double-counted and so on.

One problematic Messianic obstacle for Matthew's genealogy is the curse of Jeconiah. Reported in Jeremiah 22:24-30, this is where God cursed Jeconiah and all his descendents ("Record this man as if childless, a man who will not prosper in his lifetime, for none of his offspring will prosper, none will sit on the throne of David or rule anymore in Judah"). This rather puts paid to Messianic claims derived through Matthew's claimed lineage since Jesus is clearly of the offspring of Jeconiah. Some apologists claim that the curse was limited to Jeconiah's lifetime whilst others claim that Jesus is disqualified as an ancestor with Messianic properties. Thus both Matthew and Luke have issues and perhaps they were each trying to divert their respective lineages around the obstacles, but in so doing created further impediments to a successful Davidic and Messianic heritage.

The accuracy of Matthew's list is clearly not important since counting the years from the birth of Jeconiah (616 BCE) to Jesus as thirteen generations, one has an *average* generation of almost fifty years, which is somewhat far-fetched in those times. In Old Testament passages, such as Ezra 7:1-5, there is precedent for abridging genealogies as Matthew seems to have done.

Matthew also appears, possibly, to have included some women, though not matriarchal women such as Sarah or Rebecca. One would think he includes Mary at the end in reference to the virgin birth.

What best explains the differences between the two Gospel genealogies? It is interesting that not only do they disagree with each other in the lineages going back to David, but more amazingly, they disagree with the father of Joseph! Augustine of Hippo, an early bishop and highly important theologian, thought that the inconsistencies in the genealogies were so crucial as to, indeed, require harmonising and explaining.[1]

One common explanation as to the issue of Joseph having two fathers is that he really did have two fathers—one legal, and one natural. This is something that was first put forward by third century apologist Julius Africanus (who claimed it for the differences in the entire lists) who called on the application of Levirate marriage laws. This happens if a man dies leaving a childless widow. It was then law that the man's brother married the widow and their first resulting son was seen as the child of the dead man.

Another suggestion for the differences in the lists is that Matthew's represents a genealogy through Joseph whilst Luke's is through Mary. This is a poor attempted harmonisation, especially since Luke's opening was "Jesus Himself was about thirty years of age, being, as was supposed, the son of Joseph, the son of Eli". The other rather obvious issue with this theory is that one genealogy is massively longer than the other, which just makes it chronologically incoherent.

Charles Foster, as a devoted Christian himself (and a lawyer), takes this tack (2007, p. 14-15):

> We have to learn to live with the fact that scripture doesn't, on its surface, tell a completely consistent story…
>
> This is a million miles from flaccid, anaemic liberalism, and is based on a much higher view of scripture than literalism. It's no accident that literalism, which makes scripture literally unbelievable, is rubbished in the opening lines of the story of Jesus…
>
> How did the discrepancies between the genealogies arise? I don't know and nor does anyone else.

Whilst this is a refreshing and honest approach, it does seem like there is unfinished and uncomfortable business here. As

---

[1] In *Contra Faustum (Reply to Faustus), Book III*

he admits, the fact that these lists don't even agree with the Old Testament is telling and probably hints at the fact that accuracy wasn't at the forefront of their concerns. I would go along with this. However, it does open up a whole can of worms in the classic manner that if the writers are being free and easy with historical fact here (without necessarily being too explicit about it) then where else are they doing this? Apologists, whenever they find problems with biblical texts, claim that the writers were being symbolic, or similar. However, with texts which don't present problems on the face of it, how can we be sure that they are not symbolic, or know that they don't, in fact, harbour historical truth? The simple answer is we can't and don't know. It is a form of cherry-picking or special pleading by not applying a consistent approach across a broader spectrum of accounts and narratives.

So what can we possibly conclude from this mish-mash of theories and harmonisations, problems and inconsistencies? The Gospel writers, in all probability, had no great desire to fulfil historical accuracy; they had an agenda. The problem is that no one can quite work it out. If the intention, as many think, is to highlight the Messianic qualities of Jesus, to rubber-stamp his divine authority, and this authentication is itself in some way fabricated, then in what way should we take it as 'Gospel Truth' that Jesus does have such Messianic qualities, such Davidic heritage? I find it very hard to be convinced by a symbolic mechanism to highlight a supposedly historic truth which is itself fabricated. There is an incoherency here which does not sit well.

Therefore, I believe Foster is right in claiming the reasons are unknown. He is wrong, though, in believing that it does not damage biblical claims of Jesus' Davidic or Messianic heritage.

48

5 - To Bethlehem or not to Bethlehem...

Bethlehem is a very important place for the average Christian. It is the birthplace of Jesus. But it is more than that, it is the birthplace of the predicted Messiah, whether Jesus existed or not. For Jews and Christians alike, Bethlehem was touted as 'the place to be born' if you had any hopes of achieving Messianic greatness. For an evangelising writer who believes and / or wants other people to believe that Jesus is the one to follow, the one Messiah that everyone had been waiting for, then Bethlehem is a prerequisite for being the birthplace of Jesus. Through the announcements of the Bible itself, Jesus has to be born in Bethlehem or the prophecies are wrong, or indeed Jesus is invalidated as the true Messiah. Having said this, a case can be made for the fact that this Bethlehem prophecy may just be a contrived and poor reading of the Old Testament. We shall return to this later.

So what are these prophecies? The main offending verse is Micah 5:2 which states:

"But as for you, Bethlehem Ephrathah,
Too little to be among the clans of Judah,
From you One will go forth for Me to be ruler in Israel.
His goings forth are from long ago,
From the days of eternity."

Let us remind ourselves of how this fits in with what Luke says of Bethlehem (2:4):

Joseph also went up from Galilee, from the city of Nazareth, to Judea, to the city of David which is called Bethlehem, because he was of the house and family of David,

1 Samuel 16 tells of how Samuel, a prophet, went to Bethlehem to anoint the king-to-be, on the behest of God. Samuel doesn't expect it to be the youngest of the children of Jesse, a mere shepherd, but David it was and he was to be the great king.

49

Jesse, being a 'Bethlehemite', would imply that David was one too.

The first issue with the Micah quote is that it is a mistranslation to claim that the Messiah must be born in Bethlehem since the context and the grammar actually mean that one should conclude, as D.F. Strauss in *The Life of Jesus* (1860, p. 159) does, as follows:

> ...the entire context show the meaning to be, not that the expected governor who was to come forth out of Bethlehem would actually be born in that city, but only that he would be a descendent of David, whose family sprang from Bethlehem.

So Matthew and Luke, in using this as a prophetic basis for establishing Davidic heritage, mistranslate the prophecy and feel that they need to get Joseph and Mary to Bethlehem so that Jesus could be born in the place so apparently prophesied. If Jesus had been born in Nazareth, he still would have fulfilled the prophecies utilised by the Gospel writers.

If we look at the potential theological contrivances in the fulfilment of the prophecy that sees the Messiah being born in the 'city of David' in light of the added evidence of the genealogies, then it is hard not to be cynical. With a faulty and clearly manufactured set of family trees which rely on some dodgy usages of the Old Testament and genealogy, a shadow is cast upon the idea that Bethlehem, as a birthplace, is not only prophesied, but seemingly fulfilled.

It is not only the apparent shoehorning of Jesus into a Bethlehem prophecy but the plethora of other issues that cause a sceptic to doubt the veracity of Bethlehem being Jesus' birthplace. Let us look at all of the evidence which points to the notion that Jesus might well have been born elsewhere.

Firstly, there is a serious lack of mention of Bethlehem in *any* other writing in the New Testament. Although absence of evidence is often claimed (by Christians) as not being evidence of absence, it is hard to deny the force of the lack of mention of Bethlehem. The Gospels of Matthew and Luke are the *only* places in which it is mentioned. Neither do Mark, John, and importantly, nor does Paul corroborate the claims of the other two. It gets slightly more problematic for those who are pro-Bethlehem in that it seems that Jesus was born in Nazareth.

Paul is at times understood to be writing, in his letters, to people very interested in the Jewishness of Jesus. If he knew that Jesus was born in Bethlehem and of the Davidic line, you would have thought this would have been a superb mechanism which Paul could have used to argue such Jewishness. Sadly, this evidence is lacking.

The Gospel of Mark seems to indicate that Jesus was born in Nazareth. Mark makes no mention, other than Jesus being from Nazareth, of any other place that Jesus could be associated with in the whole of his Gospel. Mark 1:9 declares, "Jesus came from Nazareth in Galilee and was baptized by John in the Jordan." Throughout the Gospel, when visiting elsewhere, such as Capernaum (Mark 1:21-28), he is referred to as Jesus of Nazareth. More damaging, perhaps, is the idea in Mark 6 where he returns to Nazareth and this is referred to as his "hometown" (6:1). This is compounded as later in that same episode Mark has Jesus *himself* saying (6:4), "A prophet is not without honor except in his hometown and among his own relatives and in his own household." There seems to be little dispute in Mark's writing that Jesus hailed form Nazareth.

In common vernacular and biblical terms, it is no coincidence that Jesus is known famously as 'Jesus of Nazareth' and not 'Jesus of Bethlehem'! It seems to me that it is more probable that Jesus was known as Jesus of Nazareth before the Gospels were written so that this title could not realistically be dropped. But since the writers needed Jesus to be born in Bethlehem it was a case of either getting him (i.e. Joseph and Mary) from there to Bethlehem and back again or living in Bethlehem at the birth and then moving to Nazareth, Luckily, the Gospels have both options. Nothing like covering all the bases!

And this leads us onto another issue: Luke and Matthew differ on where Joseph and Mary lived before the birth of Jesus. As Luke 2:3-5 says:

> And everyone was on his way to register for the census, each to his own city. Joseph also went up from Galilee, from the city of Nazareth, to Judea, to the city of David which is called Bethlehem, because he was of the house and

family of David, in order to register along with Mary, who was engaged to him, and was with child.

Clearly, Luke has Jesus living in Nazareth and having to go to Bethlehem as a result of it being "his own city" (more on this later) and having to attend a census (more on this later, too!). Matthew, on the other hand, has this to say (Matthew 1-2):

> Now the birth of Jesus Christ was as follows:
> ...
> Now after Jesus was born in Bethlehem of Judea...

So, although there is no explicit explanation of where they lived, it is implied by the manner in which the account is given. However, the admission that they had not lived in Nazareth before comes in Matthew 3:21-23 after the family have lived in Egypt for what was probably a couple of years:

> So Joseph got up, took the Child and His mother, and came into the land of Israel. But when he heard that Archelaus was reigning over Judea in place of his father Herod, he was afraid to go there. Then after being warned by God in a dream, he left for the regions of Galilee, and came and lived in a city called Nazareth. This was to fulfil what was spoken through the prophets: "He shall be called a Nazarene."

This spells out a clear contradiction between Matthew and Luke—they could not agree on where Joseph and Mary lived before the birth. Both writers had to harmonise two points: that Jesus had to be born in Bethlehem, and that he had to live in Nazareth. And they both do this in completely different ways. Luke uses a census and a need to go to the town of one's ancestors, whilst Matthew uses an escape to Egypt and the notion that Bethlehem was too dangerous to live in, and the need to fulfil the 'Nazarene' prophecy. It is worth noting here that another of Herod's sons was ruling Galilee, and yet this did not stop the family moving there. Is this a case of double standards? The difference between the two Gospels is one of those contradictions that, to me, is fairly terminal for the narratives as a whole. Such a fundamental difference, and such dichotomous mechanisms for getting Jesus from A to B, shows at least one, and probably both, accounts to be indefensibly spurious. As Foster, (2007, p. 60) says:

> The discrepancies [between Luke and Matthew] are real and dramatic. That means that it cannot be argued with a straight face that Matthew and Luke collaborated or had a common source.

This implies that many apologists don't argue many of their harmonisations with a straight face. With the mounting evidence, I can see why. Apologists do, however, use various methods to get themselves out of this corner.

To begin with, apologists will tackle the absence of evidence claim (from the writings of John, Mark and Paul) as not proving anything, per se. Furthermore, it is claimed that Paul would be trying to play down the Jewishness of Jesus in dealing with the many Gentiles in the growing religion. The absence from the other two Gospels is often put down to the notion that writers simply did not have the same source(s) as Matthew and Luke, or themselves did not want to play to Jesus' Jewishness.[1]

Another tack is that just because Bethlehem offers itself as a very important theological device in validating Jesus' authentic Davidic and Messianic qualities does not mean that it is not true that he was born there. Maybe that theological detail isn't true, or maybe it is, but that does not, by default, make the claim that Jesus was born in Bethlehem false. Well, no, but on balance of evidence, the probability is very low. Taking into account the many inconsistencies between the Gospels, and the places in which there is at least one of the accounts telling a falsity, it does push the conclusion towards the improbable end of the spectrum.

Foster analogises a liberal approach to Matthew's use of prophecy fulfilment by using Matthew 21. In this account, since the prophet Zechariah in the Old Testament had prophesied that the king enter Jerusalem on a donkey and a colt, Matthew sees that this must be fulfilled by Jesus, and as a result states (Matthew 21:6-7):

---

[1] Foster (2007, p. 60)

> The disciples went and did just as Jesus had in-
> structed them, and brought the donkey and the colt, and
> laid their coats on them; and He sat on the coats.

However, Mark and Luke see this as nonsense and have him only riding on a donkey. Foster argues that it is obvious that Matthew is factually wrong here, since Jesus wouldn't have been riding two animals at once, but does it mean he didn't enter Jerusalem at all? Foster says a resounding no (2007, p. 61-62). The problem with his analogy is this. Firstly, he shows corroborating evidence that Matthew's factual claims (at least of prophecy fulfilment) are simply wrong. They didn't happen *as was claimed*. Matthew is playing fast and loose with facts here; as mentioned before, where else is he doing this where it is not so obvious? Secondly, and more importantly, it is a false analogy. The point is not to say whether Jesus was born at all[1] (as in, entered Jerusalem in Matthew 21), but to say he was not born in the way claimed (as in, he did not enter Jerusalem in the way claimed).

Thus Foster fails in defending the genealogies and birth narratives in the way intended. What Matthew's inconsistent writing does seem to evidence is that Jesus was not born *in the way claimed* by Matthew (and Luke). It seems Jesus was not born a virgin, did not have a genealogy routed through David, was not born in Bethlehem and so on. What we could have left is this: Jesus was born. But many proponents of the 'truth' of the narratives of Jesus' birth appear to be oblivious to this.

Other attempts to harmonise the problematic accounts include claiming that Matthew didn't explicitly say that Bethlehem was always their home, and that they could have lived elsewhere before. This is possible to grant, but the fact that they then decided to move to Nazareth after Egypt clearly shows that they *hadn't* lived in Nazareth before. So the contradiction with Luke remains unanswered.

Another claim is a result of the tradition that Jesus was born in a cave close to Bethlehem. The earliest extant proof of this comes from 2nd Century Justin Martyr's writing. He put forward

---

[1] Though one can argue for the entire mythology of Jesus, I am not doing so here.

that, after finding no space in the inns of the village, Jesus was born in a nearby cave. Again, in his *Dialogue with Trypho* (chapter LXXVIII):

> Joseph took up his quarters in a certain cave near the village; and while they were there Mary brought forth the Christ and placed Him in a manger, and here the Magi who came from Arabia found Him.

The tradition is still alive and kicking as there is now *The Church of the Nativity* built over the supposed cave. The idea is that there must be some basis for this tradition, and that basis could well be the truth of the claim. Conversely, critics claim that it was invented by Martyr who could have been basing it on an obscure Isaiah passage (33:16):

> He will dwell on the heights, His refuge will be the impregnable rock; His bread will be given him, His water will be sure.

The "impregnable rock" is thus referring to the cave. The counter-claim is that the reference was too obscure and that Martyr was too good an apologist for that, with no interest in having Jesus born in a cave, being that it was dangerously close to the birth legend of Mithra, as discussed. On the other hand, this could be precisely why he might want to claim thus, in order to trump Mithraism.

There is an early Armenian version of Matthew which includes the cave, as do many early writers after Martyr, showing it as a popular belief. Perhaps, it has been claimed[1], this represented the original story which was later adapted to avoid confusion with Mithraism. This is certainly an interesting theory which is, unfortunately, fairly hard to investigate further.

Early church father Jerome claims that the cave became a shrine to Adonis after it was thought to be the birthplace of Christ.

---

[1] D.L. O'Leary, British Coptologist and lecturer at Bristol University (who published a number of Coptic liturgical manuscripts), in *Studies in the Apocryphal Gospels of Christ's Infancy.*

The Romans, he claims, did this to annoy the Christians. However, more critical scholars think the opposite[1]:

> Modern mythologists, however, reverse the supposition, insisting that the cult of Adonis-Tammuz originated the shrine and that it was the Christians who took it over, substituting the worship of their own God.

In effect, the two biblical accounts hardly give us reason enough to conclude without some serious doubts that Jesus was born in Bethlehem. It fits into some neat prophecies, and has caused the two accounts to diverge somewhat critically. The best defence seems to come from a later writer, Martyr, for which we have no source, and which involves counter-claims (and ends up being little better than any other claim, and certainly no better than sceptical analyses). The ice upon which the narratives stand, it seems, is getting thinner.

---

[1] Marcello Craveri, an Italian biblical scholar, in *The Life of Jesus*, (1967, p.36)

6 – Quirinius vs. Herod and the ten year gap

One of the most famous inconsistencies between the two Gospels arises from the use of two people, the governor Quirinius and the King Herod. These two people, Quirinius being employed by Luke, and Herod being employed by Matthew, have caused much consternation over the years and not a little attempted ad hoc harmonisation.

Let us remind ourselves of the context. Luke has this to say of Quirinius (2:1-3):

> Now in those days a decree went out from Caesar Augustus, that a census be taken of all the inhabited earth. This was the first census taken while Quirinius was governor of Syria. And everyone was on his way to register for the census, each to his own city.

This seems to be a fairly explicit statement that Quirinius is alive and well, governor of Syria, and ordering a census that came directly from Rome and the Emperor Caesar Augustus. Matthew, on the other hand, claims this (2:1-4):

> Now after Jesus was born in Bethlehem of Judea in the days of Herod the king, magi from the east arrived in Jerusalem, saying, "Where is He who has been born King of the Jews? For we saw His star in the east and have come to worship Him." When Herod the king heard this, he was troubled, and all Jerusalem with him. Gathering together all the chief priests and scribes of the people, he inquired of them where the Messiah was to be born.

This, too, is an explicit statement that Herod was in charge of Judea at the time of Jesus' birth. Thus using simple logic we can deduct that, at the time of Jesus' birth, both the census of Quirinius took place and Herod lived. However, this is extremely problematic since we know that the census took place in 6 CE and Herod died in 4 (or 5) BCE. This is a gap of *at least ten years*! It is at least ten years since if Herod was alive at the time of Jesus' birth and we know he ordered a massacre and suchlike (all of which would have taken some time), then we know he would have survived for some time around this moment and after the birth. This is quite a long period of time to have as some anomaly. On the face of it, either one or both of the Gospel authors are lying. They are simply claiming things as facts which are impossible.

In this section I am mainly going to look at the claim that Jesus was born at the time of Herod the Great since the census and Quirinius claims are looked at in greater detail in Part 3 of the book. With regard to Matthew's reference to Herod, it must be noted that Herod had three sons; all called Herod—Herod Archelaus, Herod Antipas and Herod Philip (as well as many other sons). We are sure that Matthew was referring to Herod the Great (the father) because he later states, after the death of Herod, when Joseph and family have fled to Egypt and look to come back:

> But when he heard that Archelaus was reigning over Judea in place of his father Herod, he was afraid to go there.

This means that Matthew was definitely referring to Herod the Great being ruler during Jesus' birth.

The standard Christian response here is to question the sources for our knowledge of when Herod died and for who was in charge for the census and when it was ordered. Let us look, then, at how we have come to think that Herod died in 4 BCE.

The famous contemporary Jewish historian Josephus provides much of the evidence for the timing of Herod's death. He claims that Herod came into power in 37 BCE and that he ruled for 34 years until his death, therefore making his death in around 4 BCE. In his *Jewish Antiquities* Book XXVII chapter 6 he declares that shortly before he died there was a lunar eclipse. This eclipse was originally thought to be the one of 13th March 4 BCE which would put Jesus as being born before that. A lunar eclipse in 5 BCE allows more realistic time for events claimed in historian Josephus' writing to take place and is possibly a more likely scenario. This eclipse was also total instead of partial, which the one of 4 BCE was. Some scholars now argue that the eclipse could have been later[1] and conclude that Herod actually died closer to 1 BCE, but these are in the great minority, the motivation of which seems to be to try to get Matthew out of this issue. It must be noted that eclipses were often used to signify important events and may not have been entirely accurate.

Let us look to see who was in charge of Syria at the time of Herod's death. Josephus, again, helps us out:

> ... as also how our people made a sedition upon Herod's death, while Augustus was the Roman emperor, and Quintilius Varus was in that country[2]

Josephus further verifies this with other mentions of Varus and Herod simultaneously:

> Now Varus, the president of Syria, happened to be in the palace [at this juncture]; so Antipater went in to his father, and, putting on a bold face, he came near to salute him. But Herod stretched out his hands, and turned his head away from him, and cried out, "Even this is an indication of a parricide, to be desirous to get me into his arms, when he is under such heinous accusations. God confound thee, thou vile wretch; do not thou touch me, till thou hast cleared thyself of these crimes that are charged upon thee. I appoint thee a court where thou art to be judged, and this Varus, who is very seasonably here, to be thy judge..."[3]

So this tells us that Matthew cannot be right in his claim that Herod was alive at the time of Jesus' birth since Luke claims that Quirinius was governor of Syria at the time. We know from Josephus that Quintilius Varus was governor of Syria at the time of Herod's death.

---

[1] E.g. Steinmann (2009). See Carrier (2011 6th edition) for a refutation of this position.

[2] Preface of *The War of the Jews*, 1.9-10

[3] Ibid, 1.617 which continues to talk of dealings with the Herods and Varus up to 1.639. This is also confirmed in 2.66-80 where Varus remains in charge after the death of Herod the Great.

Some Christians will call Josephus' historical accuracy into question. For example, W.F. Albright, the famous Christian archaeologist, claimed "how inaccurate Josephus generally was in details"[1]. Josephus, though, given the context, can be described as a fairly accurate historian in many ways. His inaccuracies are most often concerned with exaggeration of numbers[2]. Some of these can be put down to copyist errors, but some scholars do try to focus on such discrepancies. In *The Credibility of Josephus*, Magen Broshi of the Israel Museum[3] states:

> Undoubtedly, the source of much of Josephus's accurate data was the Roman imperial commentaries, the *hupomnemata*, specifically mentioned by him three times in his later works...
>
> It has not been our intention here to prove that he is always exact or correct in every statement, but to show that his data are in many instances accurate, and that they stem from reliable sources to which he had access from the very beginning of his literary career.

These references we have to Herod and Varus are not mere numbers, or even dates, in a sense. These are multiple accounts as to the fact that Varus and Herod simultaneously existed and ruled (or in Herod's case, died). Furthermore, we also know the dates, through Roman records and other sources[4], of who the governors of Syria were. The list is as follows:

13/12 – 10/9 BCE Marcus Titius
10/9 – 7/6 BCE   Gaius Sentius Saturninus
7/6 – 4 BCE   Publius Quintilius Varus

---

[1] W. F. Albright, JOR 22 (1931-32), p. 411.
[2] Cohen (1979) p. 233
[3] The article first appeared in *Journal of Jewish Studies: Essays in Honor of Yigael Yadin* in 1982 by the Oxford Centre for Postgraduate Hebrew Studies and can be found at http://www.centuryone.com/josephus.html (retrieved 15/01/2012)
[4] E.g. Strabo, Velleius, Tacitus and Josephus.

4 – 1 BCE Unknown, probably Lucius Calpurnius Piso[1]
1 BCE – 4 Gaius Julius Caesar Vipsanianus
4 – 5   Lucius Volusius Saturninus
6 – 12   Publius Sulpicius Quirinius
12 – 17   Quintus Caecilius Metellus Creticus Silanus

Thus based on this list derived from multiple accounts, we can surmise that Herod definitely ruled no later than 4 BCE. We can also use evidence of coinage for Varus' rule which end in 4 BCE.

To further state the case, Josephus (*Jewish War* 1.670) has Herod's son Archelaus ending his reign, which started at the death of his father Herod the Great's death, after ten years of rule in 6 CE. This means that his father must have died in 4 BCE or shortly before. Archelaus' dates are confirmed by another source, Roman historian Cassius Dio in his *Roman History* (55.27.6). Before it is suggested that he merely got his information off of Josephus, it is apparent that he did not use Josephus as his source since he claims that he does not know why Archelaus was deposed which he would have known if he had read Josephus (even to the point of accusing the wrong people—his brothers). He also calls him by a different name (Herod the Palestinian rather than Archelaus). If you still have any doubt, this is corroborated by Roman coinage from Judea[2].

The problem with some apologists, such as Jack Finegan in his *Handbook of Biblical Chronology* (1998), is that to establish a later death for Herod (such as based on a later lunar eclipse) they have to throw out all the other evidence which supports an earlier date which make it entirely unlikely and ad hoc. For example, it would mean that Varus must have had an unusually long governorship. But since we are fairly certain that Varus' governorship ended in 4 BCE, this would be highly improbable and against *known* evidence. It is a dangerous pastime to try to manipulate a conclusion with known data since, though the conclusion may be

---

[1] See Dabrowa (1998) p. 22-26 for evidence of Piso governing in 1 BCE and that Varus had finished his rule in 4 BCE. Also, see Carrier (2011, 6th Ed) for such a defence and its sources.

[2] See no 4954 A.M. Burnett in *Roman Provincial Coinage*.

desirable, the use (or brushing under the carpet) of the known data is not desirable. As Richard Carrier (2011) says:

> So the case for any date earlier than 5 B.C. or later than 4 B.C. for Herod's death is simply untenable in every respect.

Apologists such as Finegan have tried many different angles, some of which are too ad hoc and contrived to even mention here, and so I will refer you to the excellent essay of Richard Carrier's, *The Date of the Nativity in Luke*, which covers multiple arguments in an emphatic and well-researched manner.

To conclude this section, it seems to be irrefutable, given the evidence, that Herod the Great died in either 4 or 5 BCE. The evidence comes from Josephus, Dio and coinage, as well as Roman records of governorship of Judea. Just taking Josephus alone, the various accounts and claims he makes are considerably interwoven with other facts. It is not good enough to simply say that he might have been inaccurate and got his dates wrong since the interconnectedness would make such a claim of inaccuracy affect a whole web of events. There would simply be no reason to throw out this positive evidence unless you have an agenda set against the implications that such a date would give. It is far more probable that, in this particular case, Josephus is correct and this is born out by further corroborated sources such as Dio and coinage.

Therefore, it is safe to say that Herod did indeed die in 4 or 5 BCE and that if Jesus was born at this time, any claims of a census coinciding with this timeframe would need some serious investigation. On the face of it, the contradiction between Luke and Matthew still clearly stands.

PART 3 – THE CENSUS

And this brings us neatly on to the topic of the census. There are so many complex claims with regard to the census and so many attempted harmonisations which involve moving, reinterpreting or changing the ordinary understanding of the census that the now famous piece of Roman bureaucracy clearly requires its own section.

As far as apologists are concerned, many and legion are the attempts to reconcile the two Gospels from a variety of established corners. I can understand why apologists feel the need to firmly establish the historicity of their claims about the census. If the census in Luke is proven to be false (as in not coinciding with the birth or similar), then it follows that Luke has lied about the motivation for Joseph to go to Bethlehem. Without this, the birth in Bethlehem is called into question which means that Jesus is perhaps not of the Davidic line; that the prophecies were incorrect; that the Magi and the Shepherds quite probably never visited and so on until the whole house of cards comes tumbling down. The ramifications of this are that Luke is not to be trusted. As mentioned before, if this passage (quoted as fact) is demonstrably wrong, then what other passages are veracious and what are false? This is a miracle claim about Jesus. What, then, of all of the other miracle claims Luke makes about Jesus? Where and how do we draw the line as to what is fact and what is fiction?

While I believe I have established beyond any reasonable doubt that Herod died in 4 or 5 BCE, it can still be claimed that the census did not take place in 6 CE or suchlike and that it is this Lucan claim which can be massaged to fit with Matthew's Herodian date.

Glenn Miller, who has a website called *A Christian Think-tank* devoted to answering tough issues and inconsistencies in the Bible (like how slavery can be countenanced by God), turns his hand in several articles to dealing with the many nativity issues.

He claims[1] that the census referred to in Luke under Quirinius was not the one of 6 CE, but was one where Quirinius was "a co-ruler with the governor of Syria (the somewhat inept Quintilius Varus) or at least placed in charge of the 14-year census in Palestine". Both of these points will be dealt with later. My point to mention here is that, as with his later comment "The census was due in 8-7 BC" (was it?) and his claim that just because there is no evidence for a world-wide census, doesn't mean there wasn't one, go to show that there is a propensity for apologists to merely assume and assert harmonisations in the desperate hope that they will suffice to negate all such problems. A mere assertion that Imperial Rome had 14 year cyclical censuses is simply incorrect.[2] And yet the casual reader of such a piece would be unaware of this, as Miller confidently assumes this as a fact without any corroborating evidence. And to think that no one in the judicious record-keeping Roman Empire would record or reference the biggest co-ordinated census in history is staggering. Such an absence of evidence *is* evidence of absence[3], or at least casts serious doubts over the claims of Luke. More on this to follow.

And so any mention of the census naturally involves dealing at some depth with the governor Quirinius since Luke clearly and explicitly connects the two. It is to Quirinius to whom I will first turn.

---

[1] Miller, "On an objection about Luke, Quirinius, and Herods:"

[2] Miller later states that we know Egypt had a 14 year cycle, and that is it. As we shall see later, it in no way follows that the rest of the Roman Empire did. There were local Egyptian reasons for this.

[3] Miller, in the same article, with rather a large portion of special pleading, claims that the argument from silence *can* work, but not in this case... As he admits, the primary reason that he thinks that there was such a census is because Luke said so.

6 – Quirinius was twice the governor anyone else was...

Naturally, in order for Luke's claims to warrant any truth value, we must establish if Quirinius was, in fact, governor of Syria. Let's remind ourselves of the fateful Lucan words (2:1-6):

> Now in those days a decree went out from Caesar Augustus, that a census be taken of all the inhabited earth. This was the first census taken while Quirinius was governor of Syria. And everyone was on his way to register for the census, each to his own city. Joseph also went up from Galilee, from the city of Nazareth, to Judea, to the city of David which is called Bethlehem, because he was of the house and family of David, in order to register along with Mary, who was engaged to him, and was with child. While they were there, the days were completed for her to give birth.

This is explicit. Caesar Augustus decreed a census. It was the first census under the governorship of Quirinius in Syria. Many apologists see the issue with the ten year gap and try to claim, amongst other things, that Quirinius must have ruled twice, and that the recorded census of 6 CE was, indeed, a second census and that a first census took place earlier, in the reign of Herod, under some alternate Quirinius rule. This is the claim that I will be looking at in this section, concluding that the traditional, obvious and historically corroborated date of Quirinius' governorship is the one that should be taken as fact.

As mentioned in the previous section, we know that Quintilius Varus was in charge from 7 BCE until the death of Herod (4 BCE). The sources for this are Tacitus, Velleius and Josephus.[1] It might be wise to refer back to the list of Roman governors in the previous section. Thus on the face of it, the governors are well

---

[1] Velleius 2.117.2; Tacitus, *Historiae* 5.9.2; Josephus, *Jewish War* 1.617-39 & 2.66-80, *Jewish Antiquities* 17.89-133, 17.221-23, 17.250-98

attested, and Quirinius fits in at 6 CE. The position of governor could only be given to people who had held the political title of consul—two were elected to this political office in the Republic each year. Quirinius was a consul in 12 BCE and thus he could not have served as governor in Syria before that. Therefore, to fit Quirinius in around this time means massaging Jesus' timeline and playing around with the governorship of Marcus Titius (13-10 BCE). The main problem for Quirinius having an earlier governorship is that it is simply not attested anywhere. There is no evidence *for* it.

More devastating for the double ruling theory is that in no province anywhere in the Roman Empire, and at no time in Roman history, did any governor ever serve twice. It is remarkably ad hoc to suggest that Quirinius served twice just to fit the census timeframe in with the life of Herod! In Tacitus' *Annals* (3:48), the historian gives an obituary for Quirinius and yet this is not mentioned there.

For Christians to hold such an improbable theory they must be able to bring something to the evidentiary table or stand accused of inventing theories to fit conclusions with no basis whatsoever. Often[1], reference is made to an inscription named *Lapis Tiburtinus*, which is part of a funeral stone found near Rome, to support a double ruling of either Quirinius or Varus, depending on the theory. The Vatican Museum now displays it, guessing at the missing parts. All that is known of it is that it was created some time after 14 CE and the death of Augustus. The translation of the inscription is as follows:

> KING BROUGHT INTO THE POWER OF...
> AUGUSTUS AND THE ROMAN PEOPLE AND SEN-
> ATE...
> FOR THIS HONORED WITH TWO VICTORY CELEBRA-
> TIONS...
> FOR THE SAME THING THE TRIUMPHAL DECORA-
> TION...
> OBTAINED THE PROCONSULATE OF THE PROVINCE
> OF ASIA...

---

[1] For example, by Ernest L. Martin at the Associates for Scriptural Knowledge (http://www.askelm.com/index.asp)

AGAIN OF THE DEIFIED AUGUSTUS SYRIA AND
PH[OENICIA]...

For those thinking this refers to Quirinius, it does not mention his name at all, or even the then Emperor Tiberius. This alone seems terminal for the theory. We know of no second victory which Quirinius had succeeded in winning against a king which is more striking, as Richard Carrier says, "especially since a "victory celebration" was a big deal--involving several festal days of public thanksgiving at the command of the emperor."[1] Furthermore, Quirinius was not known to have governed Asia. Piso, on the other hand, *did*, as well as defeating Thracian kings twice. He may well have also governed Asia and had at least one victory celebration as alluded to in the inscription. As a result, this epitaph is highly unlikely to have belonged to Quirinius, and could well have belonged to the likes of Lucius Calpurnius Piso instead. As Carrier concludes:

> Even more importantly, this inscription does not really say that the governorship of Syria was held twice, only that a second legateship was held, and that the second post happened to be in Syria. From what remains of the stone, it seems fairly obvious that the first post was the proconsulate of Asia. This means that even if this is the career of Quirinius, all it proves is that he was once the governor of Syria.[2]

For an incredibly convoluted and contrived chronology by a Christian apologist, see Ernest L. Martin's *The Star that Astonished the World* (1991) where all known dates seem to have been massaged into a chronology that fits all the claims of the Bible with some rather ad hoc theorising, including the double governorship of Quintilius Varus which lends itself to said theorising. The same problem exists: no person is known to have governed a province twice, and there is no evidence (other than an ad hoc appeal to the Lapis Tiburtinus and its missing words) to support

---

[1] Carrier (2011)
[2] Ibid.

Varus, let alone Quirinius serving in this position twice. As Christian apologist Charles Foster (2007, p.36) himself says:

> Christian apologists often assert, with astonishing confidence, that there was more than one Quirinius, or that if there was one, that he was governor of Syria more than once... This smacks of desperation, and requires some highly imaginative handling of the evidence.

A second inscription, called the *Lapis Venetus*, gives evidence that a census took place in Syria under Quirinius. This much we know anyway, and any further conclusions from this inscription are mere suppositions. Esteemed British historian and Emeritus Professor at Oxford University, Fergus Millar, in *The Roman Near East (31 BC-AD 337)* (1885, p. 48 and 250). claims that there is good reason to believe that the census mentioned is indeed the 6 CE census as opposed to any earlier one which is unevidenced elsewhere but could harmonise the scriptures.

Perhaps more famous than the Lapis Venetus are the *Antioch Stones*. This brace of stones was found in 1912 and 1913 near Psidian Antioch (near the Turkish Lakes) and were created to commemorate Gaius Juliuus Caristanius Caesiano who was deputy duumvirate (double leader) of a city under Quirinius. It is undated though thought to date from around 11 to 1 BCE. Unfortunately, the stones were reused, but a photograph and a sketch remain. The problem for using these stones as ecidence to refer to anything to do with the governorship of Quirinius (double or otherwise) is that these refer to the rule over a city and not a province, such as Syria. As Christian author Richard Racy states, in *Nativity* (2007, p.310-11):

> Merely recording that a man served under Quirinius tells us nothing about Quirinius and no date tells us nothing about when he served...
> ... That would put the date of Quirinius' duumvirate around 2 BC, not the AD 5 date required to support Luke's account.

The city was also not in the province of Syria so it is a wonder that the stones can really be used as evidence to somehow support the Lucan narrative[1].

Another piece of 'evidence' co-opted by apologists is coinage on which microletters (incredibly small letters) are to be found. These letters elicited claims by the archaeologist Jerry Vardaman which inspired this quote from Carrier which deserves to be cited here:

> Vardaman… claimed to have discovered microscopic letters covering ancient coins and inscriptions conveying all sorts of strange data that he then uses matter-of-factly to assert the wildest chronology I have ever heard for Jesus. He claims these "microletters" confirm that Jesus was born in 12 B.C., Pilate actually governed Judaea between 15 and 26 A.D., Jesus was crucified in 21 and Paul was converted on the road to Damascus in 25 A.D. This is certainly the strangest claim I have ever personally encountered in the entire field of ancient Roman history. His evidence is so incredibly bizarre that the only conclusion one can draw after examining it is that he has gone insane. Certainly, his "evidence" is unaccepted by any other scholar to my knowledge. It has never been presented in any peer reviewed venue, and was totally unknown to members of the America Numismatic Society until I brought it to their attention, and several experts there concurred with me that it was patently ridiculous.

Apologist John McRay was one apologist who did believe Vardaman: "Jerry Vardaman has discovered the name of Quirinius on a coin in micrographic letters, placing him as proconsul of Syria and Cilicia from 11 B.C. until after the death of Herod."[2] He, in turn, in an interview with Lee Strobel, convinced Lee Strobel to the point that Strobel, TV presenter and author of the very popular and influential *The Case for Christ* (1998), found it be the

---

[1] Again, refer to Carrier (2011) which is available variously online and completely deconstructs and invalidates the use of the Lapis Tiburtinus, Lapis Venetus and the Antioch Stones by various Christian sources.

[2] McRay in *Archaeology and the New Testament*, (1991, p. 154).

clinching piece of evidence for the reliability of Luke's account.[1]
On p.101 of his book, Strobel claims:

> An eminent archaeologist named Jerry Vardaman
> has done a great deal of work in this regard. He has found a
> coin with the name of Quirinius on it in very small writing,
> or what we call 'micrographic' letters. This places him as
> proconsul of Syria and Cilicia from 11 B.C. until after the
> death of Herod.

This is interesting since it is hard to see how Vardaman is
an eminent archaeologist. Strobel did himself no favours when
admitting on a FOX TV show in the US that these coins represented "the strongest example of archaeological confirmation"
that the Bible is true.[2] Some of the claims of Vardaman are as
follows, as set out in Summers and Vardaman (1998, p. 133-4):

> In support of his position, claims of Vardaman have
> brought to light new evidence in the form of "microletters"
> on certain first century coins ... which he argues affirm Je-
> sus' public ministry in A.D. 16 and his execution in A.D.
> 21...
> Vardaman illustrates that the inscription *REX JESVS*
> is frequently scratched in microletters on a Damascene coin
> from A.D. 16

Vardaman claims (Vardaman and Yamauchi 1989, p. 70)
that "Many other coins of Damascus... also mention Jesus in
microletters". These letters cannot be seen without the help of a
magnifying glass and could only have been inscribed with some
sort of incredible, possibly diamond-tipped tool. I will list the
fundamental issues with the 'evidence' given by Vardaman (apart
from that already given):

> • He has never produced any of these coins or prop-
>   erly referenced them.

---

[1] Foster (2007, p. 38)
[2] Dec 10th 2005, John Kaisch programme on FOX.

- Coins of such an age would have literally thousands of years of wear and oxidation. Such letters would not have survived.
- Suspiciously, no photographs of these inscriptions have been published, merely his own drawings.
- Estimates of the letter size are about ½ a millimetre, throwing suspicion over how hundreds of these inscriptions could be made, let alone survive.
- He claims a coin minted in an Eastern Greek city has words in Latin when they used Greek letters.
- Vardaman uses modern Js where the letter did not exist in Latin (it was written as I)!
- He claims that a coin was minted in Damascus under the rule of Aretas IV in 16 CE but it was not ceded to Aretas until 37 CE which is actually different to how the coin is dated on its mint.
- He claims multiple references to Jesus and his titles on coins from 16 CE.
- His dating is mere assertion.
- There is no coin about Quirinius, even though it is referenced by McRay (supposedly an unpublished paper by Vardaman). The claim about Quirinius is maintained in a later lecture by Vardaman, but in relation to an inscription, not a coin.

As you can quite patently see, this 'evidence' from Vardaman (now deceased) is seemingly concocted and in my opinion should be summarily ignored. I cannot emphasise this enough.

Some Christians are proponents of the theory that Quirinius ruled at another point in time in a dual-rule with someone else. Essentially, this problem falls into the same trap as the claim that he ruled twice, separately, in that it is unprecedented in Roman history. Ernest L. Martin implores that "there was no consistent system yet worked out for the governorships of these provinces."[1]

---

[1] See Appendix 1, Martin (1991)—though with respect to a double governorship of Varus. Marchant (1980) does effectively posit this for Quirinius, though. Interestingly, I counted 9 "may"s, 5 "might"s, 4 "possibly"s, 3 "could"s and 2 "probably"s in what is a very short article! Fairly tentative to say the least.

However, in direct opposition to this point, Carrier (2011) replies that "this is argued with no evidence whatsoever, and it is flatly contradicted by the evidence we do have." There is a passage in Josephus (*Jewish Antiquities* 16.280) in which he remarks, "there was a hearing before Saturninus and Volumnius, who were in charge of Syria" to which some people appeal for precedent for a double ruling. As such, apologist Ronald Marchant in his 1980 paper "THE CENSUS OF QUIRINIUS: The Historicity of Luke 2:1-5" claims this:

> Whether Voulmnius [sic] was co-equal with Saturninus or only his chief assistant, the passage still indicates that more than one person could be "governors" or "leaders of Syria" (*twn Surias epistatountwn*). The implication of these facts is that, at least during the period with which we are concerned, we cannot confine our conclusions about who was "ruling Syria" to the list of provincial governors which scholars have compiled. The objection that Quirinius was not governor (or *legatus*) of Syria until AD 6, and that therefore Luke is in error, thus falls to the ground.

However, Josephus (*Jewish War* 1.538) clears this up with reference to another hearing: "Saturninus and the senior colleagues of Pedanius, among whom was Volumnius the procurator." Indeed, he is clearly referring to two separate positions held by these two people rather than concurrent identical positions. Moreover, Volumnius was of the equestrian class (the lower of the two aristocratic classes in Rome) and, as such, was not allowed to be a governor. This 'evidence' is dead in the water, or ironically falls to the ground itself.

A further proposal for the likes of Quirinius is that the verb used by Luke in reference to Quirinius' rule does not strictly mean 'to govern', but is a more generalised understanding of command, thus invalidating the notion that the census took place whilst Quirinius was a governor of Syria. He had been in Asia Minor fighting a war from 6 BCE through to 1 BCE. In this way, apologists[1] claim that the census could have taken place during a sort of military leadership of Quirinius before his actual governor-

---

[1] For example, Marchant (1980)

ship. This, again, has a series of problems. Firstly, Luke would not be referring to this kind of leadership to signpost when a census was held. Why would he want to signpost the census in Syria by referring to the military leader of the Roman army in Asia? The clear and obvious choice would be the governor himself. Moreover, fighting skirmishes in nearby Galatia and Cilicia does not imply a command of anything in Syria. Galatia is its own province and is obviously *not* Syria. In geographical terms, the army fighting there would have to come from the North, in Galatia, and not Syria.[1] In order for this claim to hold, a large stretch of plausibility and a dollop of generosity in reading Luke would have to be afforded.

If we return to our original problem, that in order to reconcile Matthew and Luke apologists find a need to have Quirinius governing Syria twice, are we provided with any decent evidence in support of a double-governing Quirinius? Well, simply put, no.

---

[1] See Ronald Syme (widely regarded as the greatest historian of ancient Rome of the last century) in "The Titulus Tiburtinus", *Roman Papers*, vol. 3, p.875

7 – The client kingdom issue

The date of the census is all important in establishing whether the claims of Luke have any veracity, and if so, in establishing when the census must have happened. Those who claim that Quirinius had ruled twice or that another governor was in charge of Syria during a census must face the issue of the fact that before 6 CE Judea was a client kingdom.

Quirinius took control of Judea in 6 CE as we have established. If Luke is to be believed then the census took place under Quirinius. This makes perfect sense in light of the fact that Judea, under Herod the Great and then his son Archelaus, who was deposed in 6 CE to be replaced by Quirinius, was a client kingdom. A client kingdom was a province which kept a degree of independence from the Roman Empire but who still had to pay an agreed annual tax, agreed between the two parties. These provinces usually existed at the edges of the empire, offering themselves as a natural, protective zone for the empire itself. Any tax within that state was the responsibility and interest of the rulers of that state. In this case, Herod (either one) would have had to pay an annual fee and would have extracted that in any way that he would have seen fit. A decree for a tax census, then, would simply not come from the Roman Emperor.

If a census had been decreed from the central Roman government, it would have been a notable occasion and one would expect multiple references to it from various sources. As Carrier (2011) expounds:

> There is no example of, or rationale for, a census of an independent kingdom ever being conducted in Roman history. Therefore, the census Luke describes could only have been taken *after* the death of Herod, when Judaea was annexed to the Roman province of Syria, just as Josephus describes. All attempts to argue otherwise have no merit: Luke did not mean a census before Quirinius, could not have imagined Quirinius holding some other position besides governor, and could not have mistook him for someone else.

What Carrier makes a solid case for is the fact that it makes no difference who was in charge before 6 CE because there could not have been a census. The effort of running and controlling the finances of a state like Syria meant that it was in Roman interests to let it self-govern (until things got so bad under Archelaus that they had to step back in).

Josephus himself corroborates the fact that Quirinius issued a census at the beginning of his reign. Early Christian Justin Martyr agrees with this claim in his First Apology (Chapter 34), where he states, "Now there is a village... in which Jesus Christ was born, as you can ascertain also from the registers of the taxing made under Cyrenius [Quirinius], your first procurator in Judaea." He confirms this later again in Chapter 46.

Therefore, the obvious conclusion to make is that Justin Martyr and Luke were both on the money with their clear statements that Jesus was born under the rule of Quirinius and that the census was the census of Quirinius (that is understood to be in 6 CE).

Most importantly, there is no good reason as to why a client kingdom would want to carry out a census, let alone there being no precedent. In order to claim that a census took place earlier than 6 CE, one has to jump the hurdles of Quirinius not being governor at the time, of Judea being a client kingdom and not having censuses (certainly for taxation purposes) and there being absolutely no evidence for any other census in this timeframe. A tall order, indeed. The census of 6 CE (indicated by Luke), on the other hand, was corroborated by several contemporary writers and fits in within the context of Roman and Judean history without the need for any unnecessary and ad hoc rationalisations.

Marchant (1980) uses another census to claim that there was precedent for censuses to take place in independent states, such as with the case of Apamea. This is erroneous since the only places that could qualify were not, indeed, free at the date suggested. The term "free inhabitants" does not entail a free city, such as one not under direct Roman rule. Also, reference to coins (as he used for evidence) from the city does not show an independent city since Rome allowed many cities to mint their own coins.

Moreover, the Greek translation of Luke is very clear in its meaning—this was the first census while Quirinius was governing

Syria. Any other explanation which places a census before 6 CE (with Quirinius governing) would be contravening a basic understanding of the Greek. In fact, Quirinius would not have ruled for long enough to have overseen two censuses. This implies that it was the first census, and that it happened to be under Quirinius. This makes sense not only of the Greek, but also in the context of it being decreed by Augustus.

The Greek also prohibits any understanding that the census in question took place *before* Quirinius became governor. For an analysis of the Greek here, see Carrier (2011) and his section *"Did Luke mean "Before" Quirinius?"*

Another defence used by apologists[1] is to claim that the census, in Roman times, took place around every fourteen years which means that there was a census in about 8-9 BCE, before the one of 6 CE. This means that a previous census would have happened either under the auspices of an earlier governor such as Saturninus, or an earlier rule of Quirinius. The reasons given above already render this claim impotent, but it also fails on other accounts.

Firstly, there were no cyclical empire-wide censuses until the later time of Vespasian. In two cases, Egypt and Sicily, there were more regular censuses for other reasons, but the cycles were different. At some points, there was a five year cycle of Roman citizens only, occasionally coinciding with the less frequent non-citizen census. In Augustus' reign, which wasn't short, he managed three censuses for Roman citizens at irregular intervals—around twenty years apart. Claiming a regular census for non-Roman citizens at a fourteen year interval is patently ridiculous. We would also expect censuses at fourteen year intervals *after* the one in 6 CE, for which we have no evidence. As far as provincial censuses go, there are some interesting comparisons to take. It seems the fourteen year theory may well come from the fact that the Roman rule inherited (from Cleopatra) an Egyptian system of fourteen year censuses but this was *particular* to Egypt. This was due to a certain tax being payable after reaching the age of fourteen. To assume this would be the case in Syria as well would require some serious explanation (especially since the nearest comparable tax in Syria was on women after the age of twelve).

---

[1] For example, John Elder (1960) and John McRay (1991).

Whilst on this subject, it is worth bringing up the fact that some apologists[1] claim that the census could have been a counting which took place in the time of Herod the Great and not the 6 CE census that we all know and love. This claim entails that the census was when the Roman Empire (the "People of Rome") gave an oath of allegiance to the Emperor Augustus, naming him as "pater patriae" or "Father of his Country". The problem with this explanation is that this was an oath only sworn by Roman citizens, not the general public dwelling in the provinces. As the Maranatha Church (evangelical church devoted to teaching the Bible verse-by-verse from the original languages) claims[2]:

> Since most people in Judaea and the Empire were not Roman citizens, Augustus could have decreed in 3BC that everyone should swear an oath of absolute obedience to him to accompany his award as being "Father of the Country"....
>
> It thus seems highly probable that all in the Empire registered an oath of obedience and an approval of the *Pater Patrae* [sic] to Augustus at this time and that Quirinius had been sent to the East to conduct it.

Any claim that includes the words "could" and "highly probable" in such a manner should ring alarm bells. It reflects a sense of desperation and claims founded on little or no evidence. Of course, Herod was not alive in 2 BCE either and there is no record of such an oath being taken in or around that time period in or around Judea! This theory also requires translating Luke's words in a clearly unusual way, something which a verse-by-verse Bible teaching establishment should be wary of. Luke describes nothing like an oath-swearing procedure and the vocabulary refers more obviously to a census.

---

[1] E.g. Finegan (1998) and Glenn Miller for A Christian Thinktank whose motto is the biblical quote "Critically examine everything. Hold on to the good." His piece "On an objection about Luke, Quirinius and Herods:" shows that he might not live up to that motto, relying on assumption and many of the issues pointed out here.

[2] http://www.versebyverse.org/doctrine/birthofchrist.html (retrieved 31/01/2012)

Glenn Miller also claims that the world-wide census refers to this oath-making ceremony, by deferring to Martin in Vardaman and Yamauchi (1989). He proclaims, "What this means is that we have *very, very clear evidence of an empire-wide registration* in the time frame required!" I find this fascinating and not to say a little charitable. The evidence provided is hugely problematic, conflating a census with an oath-making ceremony. This is essentially what Martin claims:

> 1) "Luke" refers to the first time Quirinius was some type of leader in Syria.
>
> 2) The "census" was actually a registration of support for the Emperor around 2-3 BCE.
>
> 3) A registration of support for the Emperor around 2-3 BCE has support from ancient authors.[1]

However, the issues with this defence of the Lucan narrative are legion, and I will pick only a few here as many will be discussed elsewhere:

> 2) The "census" was actually a registration of support for the Emperor around 2-3 BCE.
>
> 1) The Greek word used by "Luke" is never otherwise used for a "registration" of support.
>
> 2) The Greek word used by "Luke" is what is normally used for a census.
>
> 3) The registration of support for the Emperor around 2-3 BCE was only for Roman citizens. It's unlikely that Joseph and Mary were Roman citizens.
>
> 4) "Luke's" detail that Joseph was required to go to his ancestral home fits better with a census than a registration.
>
> 5) You still have different dates as per Josephus [such that] Herod the Great died [in] 4 BCE.[2]

---

[1] As set out in Errancy Wiki in the article "Luke 2:2 Holding" named so because apologist J.P. Holding uses this defence of the Lucan narrative. http://www.errancywiki.com/index.php?title=Luke_2:2_Holding (retrieved 10/03/2012)

[2] Ibid.

It is this kind of harmonisation which frustrates me in that such harmonisations don't cohere across different defences. Here, an oath-ceremony may appeal to an apologist scrabbling for potential "get-out of jail free cards" but it simply does not cut the critical mustard. To compound a sense of how any "evidence" which supports a harmonisation is good enough for some apologists, Miller concludes about the Martin oath claim, "We have positive evidence of an empire-wide decree of Augustus within a year or two of the required date". Despite this decree not being a census, Miller is happy enough to settle for something which is 'roughly at the same time'. This cannot be seen as good scholarship.

To continue to expose the weaknesses of the oath-making defence, it is fairly evident that people would *not* have had to travel to a far-off town, particularly an ancestral town, to do this (it is unlikely for a census and even more unlikely for swearing an oath). Luke's words "that a census be taken of all the inhabited earth" can only refer to a census (for an analysis of the original Greek in this context, again see Carrier 2011) as the Errancy Wiki sets out above. Without any evidence whatsoever to support such a claim (of an oath-swearing ceremony), it is hard to see why it is attractive (other than to cure a headache brought on by textual incoherence).

Consequently, it seems that the evidence clearly points to the reported notion that the census referred to in Luke *was* the census of 6 CE; that it *did* take place under Quirinius; that it *was* the first census in Syria; that as a client kingdom before this time, Syria would *not* have had a census; that Quirinius *did* only rule once; and that such a claim *is indeed* incongruent with the claim that Herod was alive and baby-killing in the name of Jesus.

For this section, I will leave you with the words of Raymond Brown (1977, p.554):

> Indeed, as regards the non-biblical "evidence", it is doubtful that anyone would have even thought about an earlier census if he were not trying to defend Lucan accuracy.

8 - Why return to an ancestral town for a census?

It is all outside the plane of reality.... It is incredible that such an unusual and disturbing proceeding, as the census spoken of by Luke must necessarily have been, should have escaped all notice in Josephus....

We will not unduly stress the peculiarity of the mode of census taking implied in our text, but it is to be noted that it is a very strange proceeding. The moving about of men and families which this reckless decree must have caused throughout the whole of the Empire is almost beyond imagination, and one cannot help wondering what advantage there could be for the Roman state in this return, for a single day, of so many scattered individuals, not to the places of their birth, but to the original homes of their ancestors. For it is to be remembered that those of royal descent were not the only ones affected by this fantastic ordinance, and many a poor man must have been hard put to it to discover the cradle of his race. The suspicion, or rather, the conviction, is borne in upon us at first sight that the editor of Luke has simply been looking for some means of bringing Joseph and Mary to Bethlehem, in order to have Jesus born there. A hagiographer of his type never bothers much about common sense in inventing the circumstances he requires.[1]

I could just leave it at that since it is a marvellous quote! However, let us look critically at the evidence, or lack thereof. One of the most difficult pieces of information to harmonise in the whole census debacle is the idea that Joseph (and betrothed) had to return to "his own city". According to Luke's genealogy, Joseph was of the Davidic line. He was, by reckoning of said genealogy, some 41 generations separated from David. A generation in the Bible was normally seen as spanning 40 years. This amount of

---

[1] Guignebert in *Jesus*, (1935, p.99-101).

time between David and Joseph was a very long time, whether a forty year generational period or not. What makes little sense here is the rationale behind what is one's "own city". Joseph has two options here:

1) the law or due procedure was to return to the town of your ancestor 41 times removed (generationally)
2) you could choose which ancestor you wanted and return to their town.

If the latter, and rather ridiculous, idea held then every Jewish man worth their salt would be trying to connect themselves to David. Bethlehem would have swollen to the size of a large city in a matter of days around the time of the census! It also raises the question as to what genealogical line you follow. Is the line in Luke only through the eldest son? Is it purely patrilineal? Five women are included in Luke's genealogy. It all seems rather random and ad hoc as to how Joseph has decided that his ancestor, whose town he must attend, is David.

What makes matters incredibly far-fetched (and downright silly, in all honesty) is the notion that you would get to completely arbitrarily select which ancestor you wanted. What I mean by this is the fact that one person (Joseph) has 2 parents, 4 grandparents, 8 great-grandparents and so on. To trace ones lineage back 41 generations, one realises that he would have to choose David out of 2,199,023,255,552 people. For male ancestors I concede that we can cut the number in half to around just over 1 trillion (these numbers would be reduced, quite clearly, by crossover and repetition of ancestors since there were obviously not that many people on earth, but the point is clear). Just on face value of doing a simple doubling calculation, we have David picked out of two trillion ancestors. Let us imagine, then, that since there would have been a great amount of crossover, the number would simply have been very large. This is staggeringly ridiculous. It is not just the arbitrariness of the selection of generations (41) but the cherry-picking of the particular ancestor. It is this same application of statistics which is used to claim that 80% of people are related to Genghis Khan, or 75% of US Presidents are related to the French King Charlemagne and Alfred the Great, as according to Burke's Peerage, the Bible of aristocratic genealogy, based in

London.[1] If this is the case, then we are left with sheer folly in apologists claiming that there was some kind of Jewish system in place by which people had to return to their "own city" by using family trees etc. The whole of Syria would have been connecting themselves to David, and would have been descending en masse on Bethlehem (given that they could actually research such a huge number of ancestors accurately).

If the first option is the case (that the law or due procedure required that one returned to their ancestral home 41 generations past or similar), then we are still within the territory of patently ridiculous. Why would a man have to return to the town of an ancestor particularly 41 generations past? Firstly, most Jewish people would simply not know this information. Secondly, even if they did, and even on a conservative migration statistic, Syria would have been sent into chaos and turmoil (as hinted at earlier).

Using some crude statistics I have worked out some figures to illustrate the problems. At an arbitrary migration factor of 1%, meaning that if you had 100 people alive in one generation then only one of them would leave town in their lives, then after 41 generations, roughly a third will have migrated of that 'original 100'. With a higher rate of 3% of a generation migrating away from their home town in their lives, then a considerable number of around 71-2% would have migrated. That means that if migration levels were around 1-3% then a sizeable chunk of the population of the area would have migrated.[2] This means that the majority of the province would have been removing themselves from the habitual abode and travelling to somewhere else to take part in a census. Even if we halved these figures, the numbers would have caused substantial issues.

---

[1] As reported by David Icke in "The Windsor-Bush Bloodlines", found at:
http://www.bibliotecapleyades.net/merovingians/merovingios_02.htm (retrieved 03/03/2012)

[2] These figures are incredibly crude in that we don't know the migration rates and it is not taking into account migration of potential incoming migrants or returning migrants etc. The point is basic—41 generations would infer a substantial amount of migration.

As former Bishop E.W. Barnes notes in *The Rise of Christianity* (1947, p. 75):

> The Romans were a practical race, skilled in the art of government. It is incredible that they should have taken a census according to such a fantastic system. If any such census had been taken, the dislocation to which it would have led would have been world-wide. Roman historians would not have failed to record it.

At the time of the census, Jews were spread out all over the known world. Imagine if you had to do that today for a census. Even with cars and public transport, the country would shut down. A majority of people would have to stop their jobs for the time it took them to move to their ancestral town to register. This would be utterly inconceivable and totally counterproductive for the very purposes of a census. Taxation is improved when productivity is higher. Something like this kind of census, requiring the workforce to shut down and take a three week census holiday, would cause the economy to go into a meltdown. Who are the people tending the fields? Who are the landlords running the inns needed to put such people up? Who are the workers stocking the market stalls? Who is out fishing? And so on. I cannot think of a more incredibly dubious and downright silly idea as a census like this. Which is why it never happened like it was claimed by Luke. As sceptic Tim Callahan states in *The Secret Origin of the Bible* (2002, p. 388):

> Since most of us are taken by the charm of the Christmas pageantry, we miss the absurdity of this situation. The Romans, while not terribly efficient in their methods of taxation, were at least pragmatic. The idea that one would have to go to their place of origin to be taxed would mean, in modern terms, that since my parents came from Kansas, I would have to return from California to that state in order to pay taxes. While we can be sure that the Romans never indulged in such foolishness — there is certainly no historical record of such a decree — even had such a policy been instituted it would not have affected Judea.

This is countered extremely often by apologists (so often that there is no need to reference it other than Marchant below) by appealing to a census which took place in Egypt. I have to admit extreme annoyance with this tactic, and it is employed by many revered apologists. The census in question took place in 104 CE. As Marchant (1980) states:

> We do have one historical parallel, found in a papyrus copy of an edict of C. Vibius Maximus (c AD 104), *eparch* of Egypt. This order (see Appendix) was issued to prepare the people for an upcoming census and reminded them that everyone who was away from "his own place" was required to return home for purposes of the census. Although we cannot say that the Egyptian procedure necessarily held for Palestine, it is clear that it was at least a permissible option for the *praefect* to use in taking a census.

The problem is that this is not a permissible option and should not be used as a precedent (even if it did happen *after* the 6 CE census) since this required *itinerant workers* to return to their homes. *Not*, may I add, their ancestral homes either. This requirement was for workers who happened to be working away from their own house to return to where they lived for purposes of accuracy in taxation and so on. This has nothing at all to do with picking an arbitrary ancestor in your lineage and deciding to return to their home town. Simply put, this papyrus from the 104 CE Egyptian census should never be used to justify the Lucan narrative. It doesn't hold up to scrutiny but this does not stop Christians rolling it out in virtually every discussion about the census. In logical terms it is a false analogy and therefore fallacious.

However, the prognosis deteriorates for the theist who adheres to the notion that Joseph and Mary would have had to migrate from Nazareth to Bethlehem for such a census. To make matters worse, at the time of the 6 CE census, Judea (where Bethlehem was situated) was indeed required to take part in the census, but Galilee was not under the same requirements. Galilee was where Nazareth was situated and so Joseph would not have been required to go to Bethlehem to take part in the census. Callahan (2002, p. 388) agrees:

There was a census, however, when Quirinius was legate in Syria that is mentioned in Lk. 2:2. But, as I have already noted, in Lk. 1:5 the birth of John and Jesus is said to have taken place when Herod was king of Judea. This would be Herod the Great, who died in 4 BCE, whereas the actual census took place in CE 6, ten years later. This again is part of Luke's garbled history. Nor can this census have affected Joseph and Mary any more than if it had happened when Herod ruled Judea; for though Judea was now a Roman province, Galilee, where Nazareth is located, was still a protectorate ruled by Herod Antipas. Certainly, unless he were compelled to do so, Joseph would not have made the trek to Bethlehem.

There seems to be no reason for Joseph to be dragging his pregnant partner 80 miles for such an event. The most plausible attempt that Christians use is to claim that Joseph had family land in Bethlehem that meant he had to return from Galilee to Bethlehem for taxation purposes. Even Richard Carrier (2011) sees this as plausible:

> We can suppose that Luke believed (or wanted his readers to believe) that Joseph had family land in Bethlehem, and that this was because it was a portion of David's land, and since Jewish Law required the return of sold land every fifty years (Lev. 25:10-28), it was impossible to ever be dispossessed of it--thus, it might have seemed obvious to every Jew that any family plot could be traced to an ancient owner, even if this really wasn't the case. And as noted ... residing outside the taxed area would not exempt any landowner from taxation or the related census so long as he held any property or citizenship in the taxed region.

Carrier looks at this whole scenario as logically possible and an angle from which the theist could 'successfully' argue that Joseph had reason to travel from Galilee to Bethlehem for a census.[1] Carrier himself has translated a Greek papyrus relating to tax

---

[1] From private email exchange with Dr. Carrier.

receipts of a humble man who paid taxes on a piece of land he owned[1], showing precedent for humble landowners. Joseph could have leased the land out, for example, in order to gain income that would cover the taxes. Although a theist *can* argue this and although it might appear to make some kind of coherence, I would argue that it would be implausible to say the least.

There are three points to make here. Firstly, Luke mentions absolutely nothing about this so if he did want his readers to believe this, he is potentially being incredibly and purposefully cryptic. It just doesn't seem plausible. Carrier argues that whilst we do not have evidence from Luke that Joseph had land down in Bethlehem or some such reason to go there, it does not follow that this was not the case. Luke simply might not have had the evidence himself; he might not have been relayed the information from his sources, with the real reason being lost to history.[2] Whilst this may have happened, and one cannot prove that it did not, one can see that this is a very ad hoc approach to rationalising Joseph's movements, as Carrier himself would probably admit in playing Devil's Advocate. It seems a very long way to go, and a very long way away, to own such a piece of (hypothesised) land. The main issue, however, is that Luke *does* provide a reason for Luke to go—because Bethlehem is his ancestral town. As is argued here, this reason alone is fraught with issues, let alone positing that Luke got this reason wrong, and he actually had to go there because he owned a piece of taxable land. It is not only that this is an ad hoc reason, but that a separate reason is given in the Lucan account! Whilst landowner and labourer are not mutually exclusive titles, at least some reference to being such a landowner might be expected. We know the land, if it existed, wouldn't be worth that much since he went to register himself, rather than send a procurator. Furthermore, Jesus would stand (being the eldest son) to inherit such land, and no mention is made of it anywhere in the Gospels. One must judge such theories on levels of plausibility, which seem to be lacking in this case.

---

[1] See http://www.richardcarrier.info/papyrus/ for more information. In private emails he argued that extended families could pool resources to manage land, but that the land would be too expensive to buy for such families who would mainly rely on inheritance for land acquisition.
[2] Ibid.

As mentioned, there is no evidence to suggest that people were returning to censuses, claiming rights to ancestral land. Additionally, if Joseph did have family land in Bethlehem that he had any rights to then one might not expect him to be looking for random inns and then having his betrothed give birth in a manger (or even a cave) when he owned a piece of land in the area. It just simply doesn't add up.

Finally, the nail in the coffin for the whole census harmonisation is the idea that anyone would travel somewhere so far for a census. Censors travelled *to* towns and did not require that masses travel *to them.* A censor's main task was to conduct a census of the Roman people. This meant taking statements under oath from all male citizens, about their property. On this statement they assigned that citizen and his family to a place in the *comitia centuriata* (an assembly of people of which the richest were in the majority and who elected the censors), to a tribe and to an economic class (certainly in censuses involving Roman citizens). Also the amount of tax to be paid was established on the basis of this property. Roman censors found that accurate census taking in the provinces was a difficult task to achieve in the best of times. To make things easier, taxes were assessed as a tithe on entire communities rather than on individuals. Tax assessments in these communities fell under the jurisdiction of provincial governors and various local magistrates. As such, Joseph would have, at best, had to make a journey to Caesarea, Dora, Tiberius or any other nearby municipal settlement rather than a completely unnecessary 80 mile trek to a town in a completely different province under different rule. As German theologian Uta Ranke-Heinemann says in *Putting away childish things: the Virgin birth, the empty tomb, and other fairy tales you don't need to believe to have a living faith* (1995, p. 10):

> Under no circumstances could the reason for Joseph's journey be, as Luke says, that he was 'of the house and lineage of David,' because that was of no interest to the Romans in this context.

The sort of reasoning given to explain this by Christians is another example of coulds and mays. As one Christian source states: "It was widely known that Roman Law oftentimes permitted local Jewish customs to remain. Therefore this can be explained in this fashion."[1] *"Therefore it can be explained"?* Where is the positive evidence for this? Some things are made of cheese, therefore it can be explained that the moon could be made of cheese. Well, *maybe* but I would like to see the evidence to support such a claim. What Jewish customs required movement on *such* a grand scale? The population moving from province to province to an arbitrary ancestral home has no precedence and, importantly, no logical necessity. It makes no sense logistically, bureaucratically, economically and legally. In other words, it didn't happen as Luke claimed.

---

[1] Reverend Philip Brown in "Are the Gospels History? - The Census of Quirinius in Luke" found at:
http://christianityversusatheism.blogspot.com/2009/07/are-gospels-history-census-of-quirinius.html (retrieved 02/02/2012)

9 - Women at the census? Surely not!

If we are particularly generous, and assume that the census took place and required Joseph to attend a town of his ancestral lineage, then there are further issues that the apologist believing in the validity of the biblical accounts must overcome. Notably, there is the issue of whether or not women were required to attend censuses.

Imagine first century Judea. A census has been called. All men, for some bizarre reason, have to go back to the town where their ancestors lived 41 generations past. Now imagine every man upping and leaving for their ancestral homes. This may have taken weeks, and their businesses would have been critically disrupted. Now imagine that their wives had to come too. This would also entail any young, dependent children going too. The whole of Judea would have been in absolute turmoil. Houses would be empty up and down the country. No wonder the inns were full, no one was in their own homes! Unless, of course, they arranged some kind of behemoth house swap.

In the eyes of the Roman law, registering was for men and men only since women had no political or property rights. In *Luke*, (1993, p.106), evangelical scholar Robert Stein states:

> It is uncertain why Mary went to Bethlehem. Was it to register along with Joseph? Usually women were not required to register.

Brown (1977, p.297) claims that "the motive was not clear" as to why Mary was required to go to Bethlehem. Jane F. Garner sets out information about Roman census with regard to women in *Women in Roman Law and Society* as follows (1991, p. 49):

> Dionysius, describing the census process ... says that citizens were required to give the following information: names, monetary valuation of property, names of fathers, age, names of wives and children.

Wives were evidently not required to give any information. Roman citizens were registered by tribe and class and this registration made an exception for women. Thus in the provinces there would have even less reason for a wife to attend a census. At most, Joseph would have had to declare his marriage, but that wasn't always carried out as it was.

In the next section I will look at why Joseph might have thought it necessary to take a heavily pregnant wife 80 mile to a census that she would not have been required to attend. It seems that there were no requirements for women to attend and so the only reason can be that she went voluntarily for other reasons. Indeed, as biblical scholar Craig A. Evans asserts in *The Bible Knowledge Background Commentary: Matthew-Luke* (2003, p.51):

> Whether married or still engaged, it is not difficult to understand why Mary, despite being near to giving birth, would have preferred to accompany Joseph.

10 - Heavily pregnant? On your donkey!

As D.F. Strauss expresses (1860, p.149), in talking of various theories of why Mary ended up in Bethlehem with Joseph:

> He allows Mary to be inscribed with Joseph, but according to Jewish customs inscriptions had relation to men only. Thus, at all events, It is an inaccuracy to represent Mary as undertaking the journey, in order to be inscribed with her betrothed in his own city. Or... if we remove this inaccuracy by a forced construction of the sentence, we can no longer perceive what inducement could have instigated Mary, in her particular situation, to make so long a journey, since, unless we adopt the airy hypothesis of Olshausen and others, that Mary was the heiress of property in Bethlehem, she had nothing to do there.

Strauss is referring to various ad hoc harmonisations which proffer that Mary had obscure and unevidenced reasons to be in Bethlehem (such as inheriting some property). This reflects the desperation some feel when faced with the evidence, motivating a scramble to find any reason that comes to mind as to why the claims might be as they are.

"Her particular situation", of course, is crucial. She is heavily pregnant, of that there is no doubt. We know that the journey from Nazareth to Bethlehem would have been some 80 miles, and not on nice, modern and smooth roads. In all likelihood, the journey would have been difficult. This was either on foot, or on donkey-back. On foot, I am guessing that the walk would have lasted over a week with a heavily pregnant woman. On donkey back, you are still talking four or five days of extreme discomfort.

It would be remarkable to think that a woman in such a situation would not have been induced to give birth in transit. To make such a long journey with such strenuous pressure on the cervix would truly have defied any expectations. Such bouncy and jerky movements put undue strain on the ligaments that support the womb. A roadside birth would have certainly been the order of

93

the day. With this in mind, what sort of loving fiancé would have insisted that their betrothed make such a journey?

The most plausible attempt at providing an explanation for this is the notion that the small town of Nazareth might well have seen Mary becoming pregnant via the Holy Spirit as a rather speculative and dubious attempt to cover up an illegitimate conception. In all fairness, if someone told me over a pint in the local pub that Mary down the road was claiming she had immaculately conceived, it would be the first thing that came to my mind! In such conservative times this could have been a very dangerous time for Mary. If she had conceived illegitimately or if people thought she had, then she would be at risk of being stoned by the locals. Of course, as mentioned, there were later rumours in Jewish literature which made such claims; that Mary was raped by a Roman soldier.

The charge of illegitimacy with regard to Mary is such a major subject that Raymond Brown dedicates an entire appendix (V) to it (perhaps because he was Catholic). The Jewish writer Celsus was no fan of Jesus and claimed as much, though it is unfortunate that we only know of his work through the critiques of his work by church father Origen. This late second century accusation is also mentioned in the work of Tertullian. An early second century rabbi called Simeon ben Azzai supposedly found a genealogy dated before 70 CE which referred to Jesus as being illegitimate[1]. This became a well-established theory in Jewish literature for many hundreds of years thereafter.

Whether there is truth to this claim or not is neither here nor there for this particular point: that Mary would have had good reason to want to go to Bethlehem and escape the rumours and potential ramifications. To emotively put the point across I have heard some Christians claim that it would be a case of staying and dying in Nazareth or leaving to go to Bethlehem with Joseph.

Although this theory does have some merit, the major issue I have with it is that if Mary was in danger of having the town think her child was illegitimate and that the baby was not Joseph's then this problem would not simply disappear with a trip to Bethlehem. The collective memory of the local inhabitants of

---

[1] See Kraus in his entry "Jesus of Nazareth" in *The Jewish Encyclopaedia,* p. 170

Nazareth is unlikely to forget a potential stoning after a mere couple of weeks or even years, depending on which Gospel you adhere to. Returning *with* said child would surely re-ignite such controversies. This pretty much invalidates the apologist claim as far as I am concerned. The claims of a miraculous birth seem to go unnoticed in Nazareth for the rest of Mary's life and her irresponsible early pregnancy entirely forgotten by the people she is running away from to a census which does not require her.

A much better suggestion and one which surely must have crossed Joseph and Mary's minds would have been for Mary to have visited and stayed with her cousin (or some such female relative) Elisabeth whom she had visited before and who knew about her miraculous conception, being no stranger to that herself. This is clearly a more probable outcome and it adds to the implausibility of the apologist claims.

11 - No work for you, Joseph!

I have hinted at the notion that Joseph, in travelling the 80 miles with his betrothed, would be walking for over a week or riding on a donkey for the best part of a week, given that Mary was very heavily pregnant.

We also have some indication that they were in Bethlehem for some time: "While they were there, the days were completed for her to give birth" (Luke 2:6). These birthing days must have been extended by the time it took to wait for and be attended by their many visitors. The shepherds came and went as well as the magi. These two events, reported separately by the two Gospels, appear not to happen concurrently. This is made an even longer process because Matthew says that the magi arrived in Jerusalem after Jesus was born (and many claim that Jesus was a toddler by this time). Now according to Luke they fled to Egypt, but let us ignore that and assume Matthew's account that they returned to Nazareth. There would then be a return journey with a newborn child which one can assume took about a week.

It seems fairly clear to me that they must have spent over three weeks away from Nazareth, either on the road or in Bethlehem, in a manger. Just as an aside here, it is also pertinent to note that if one family out of the whole of the census population were unable to find accommodation, then one can assume that there were many, many families up and down Judea and surrounding areas put up in stables, barns and caves. Is this realistic? If we then take into account that Herod was looking at killing children under the age of two, then it could well be that Joseph and family spent an inordinately unrealistic amount of time away from home and job. That said, according to Matthew, Joseph and family already lived in Bethlehem. The confusion seems endless.

With so long away from home it is a serious consideration as to how a simple carpenter could afford this period of not working. Joseph was a *tekton* which translates often as carpenter though it is more likely to refer to a general contractor which could well mean a builder of some variety or similar. In any case, he would not have been a well-paid worker receiving at best two sesterces a day. To be able to take that length of time off work does leave the reader with some questions. He would have been sustaining himself, Mary, possibly a donkey and the baby Jesus with food and lodgings along the way. More importantly, he would not be receiving any income since he would not have been working for around three weeks.

In an isolated case, this would be implausible still, but acceptable. But on the scale of an entire province undergoing a census, this is nothing short of economically insane. The economy would surely have collapsed with such an absentee workforce. People's disposable incomes would have been decimated for a long time henceforth. A three week holiday today in modern Western civilisation with a comparatively huge disposable income is tough enough. In days of subsistence existences it is beyond belief.

Moreover, if we take Luke's account of proceedings, then the family definitely moved from Nazareth to Bethlehem and then moved to Egypt for probably several years. This then creates even more problems for the likelihood of a *tekton* to be itinerant for so long and be able to sustain a family on such wages. Furthermore, we simply have no evidence from the Gospels to support such a notion. This simply adds to the implausibility of the infancy narratives.

PART 4 – IT'S NOT ALL ABOUT THE CENSUS

12 - The Magi are copied from Daniel and are clearly a theological mechanism

Despite what popular culture decrees, the three wise men who visited Jesus in the manger were not kings. The word used to describe them is magi (*magoi*) and is usually understood to mean that they were astrologers / astronomers and this implies a title of wise men. We are not entirely sure that there were, indeed, three of them since this is implied from the fact that Matthew lists three gifts given to Jesus. They arrived from the East, stopping off at Herod's palace in Jerusalem on his behest. They were then sent to Bethlehem to praise the newborn king with Herod's hope that they would return to him with information:

The Visit of the Magi
[1] Now after Jesus was born in Bethlehem of Judea in the days of Herod the king, magi from the east arrived in Jerusalem, saying, [2] "Where is He who has been born King of the Jews? For we saw His star in the east and have come to worship Him." [3] When Herod the king heard this, he was troubled, and all Jerusalem with him. [4] Gathering together all the chief priests and scribes of the people, he inquired of them where the Messiah was to be born. [5] They said to him, "In Bethlehem of Judea; for this is what has been written by the prophet:
[6] 'AND YOU, BETHLEHEM, LAND OF JUDAH,
ARE BY NO MEANS LEAST AMONG THE LEADERS OF JUDAH;
FOR OUT OF YOU SHALL COME FORTH A RULER
WHO WILL SHEPHERD MY PEOPLE ISRAEL.'"

> [7] Then Herod secretly called the magi and determined from them the exact time the star appeared. [8] And he sent them to Bethlehem and said, "Go and search carefully for the Child; and when you have found Him, report to me, so that I too may come and worship Him." [9] After hearing the king, they went their way; and the star, which they had seen in the east, went on before them until it came and stood over the place where the Child was. [10] When they saw the star, they rejoiced exceedingly with great joy. [11] After coming into the house they saw the Child with Mary His mother; and they fell to the ground and worshiped Him. Then, opening their treasures, they presented to Him gifts of gold, frankincense, and myrrh. [12] And having been warned by God in a dream not to return to Herod, the magi left for their own country by another way.

It can also be said that the use of the three gifts is itself symbolic and carefully thought out by Matthew. The queen of Sheba, in the Old Testament, paid homage to king Solomon with Sheba being the southern end of the Incense Route and the source of frankincense and myrrh. Gifts good enough for King Solomon are good enough for Jesus, it would seem.

Being from the East, the magi were probably from the Parthian Empire and thus would most likely be Zoroastrians by religious persuasion. This looks to be a capitulation of Zoroastrianism to the wonder of the Almighty, to Jesus. The wise men of Zoroastrian beliefs realise that Jesus is the Almighty, and they leave the heartland of their religion to praise Jesus.

Richard Carrier, in his essay *Why I Don't Buy the Resurrection Story*, illustrates a motif in Matthew, linking Jesus with Daniel. Daniel, as an Old Testament prophet, was a very popular figure in early Christian art with whom to compare Jesus. It is worth referring to Robin Jensen's 2010 piece *Witnessing the Divine: The Magi in Art and Literature* in which it is declared:

> The magi's visit to the crib was thus their moment of conversion and the renunciation of their misguided, idolatrous practices. And so Justin reads Matthew's story as a sign to the world that Christianity was the true and pure faith... This popular interpretation is reflected in art, which

often links the three magi with the three Hebrew youths in the fiery furnace (Daniel 3) and with Daniel in the lions' den (Daniel 6) – all easterners (Daniel and the Hebrew youths lived in the Persian court) who used their gifts of prophecy, dream interpretation and perhaps even magic to resist the evil of pagan idolatry.

Let me set out a little background information about Daniel in the Old Testament. Daniel, whilst in Babylonian captivity where he remained loyal to Yahweh, was made "ruler over the whole province of Babylon and chief prefect over all the wise men of Babylon" (Daniel 2:48) by the King Nebuchadnezzar and was a prophet of great integrity. In fact, so much so, that he was a more upright and righteous man than Solomon or David who both disobeyed God. Daniel never disobeyed or argued with God. Daniel named three Babylonians (from the East) as assistant governors. The three wise men of Daniel were thrown into a fire for refusing to worship a massive statue of a Babylonian God. Nebuchadnezzar then said of this, "Look! I see four men loosed and walking about in the midst of the fire without harm, and the appearance of the fourth is like a son of the gods!" In most other translations this reads as "Son of God". Nebuchadnezzar himself has direct parallels with Herod—both disobey the will of God, both are insecure and forthright, and both order a massacre of sorts (Nebuchadnezzar the wise men and Herod the infants).

There are many parallels between the two accounts. Firstly, let me refer to Richard Carrier (2006) who points out the relationship of Daniel to Jesus both in birth and death:

> The parallels here are far too dense to be accidental: like the women who visit the tomb of Jesus, the king visits the tomb of Daniel at the break of dawn (6:19); the escape of Jesus signified eternal life, and Daniel at the same dramatic moment wished the king with eternal life (6:21; the identical phrase appears in reference to God in 6:26); in both stories, an angel performs the key miracle (Matt. 28:2, Daniel 6:22); after this miracle, the guards become "like dead men," just as Daniel's accusers are thrown to the lions and killed (6:24). Matthew alone among the Gospels ends

his story with a commission from Jesus (28:18-20), whose power extends "in heaven and on earth," to "go and make disciples of all nations" and teach them to observe the Lord's commands, for Jesus is with them "always." Curious, then, that the same author who alone creates a parallel with Daniel, is also alone in borrowing language from the same story for this commission: for King Darius, after the rescue of Daniel, sends forth a decree "to all nations" commanding reverence for God, who lives and reigns "always," with power "in heaven and on earth" (Daniel 6:25-28; the Greek phrase is identical in both cases: *en ouranôi kai epi tês gês*). The stories thus have nearly identical endings.

This sets the scene for how Matthew borrows from Daniel. The motifs and theological overtones seem to be fairly obvious to the reader, especially (as the early Jewish Christians would be) the reader who is well versed in the Hebrew Scriptures of the Old Testament. Matthew is using *Midrashic[1]* techniques to rewrite Daniel in the context of the Jesus narrative. Or more precisely, to write the Jesus narrative in the context of Daniel. Does this necessarily mean that what Matthew writes about is false? No, it doesn't. It could be that he has a set of historical events which he wants to deliver in a symbolic manner to give it historical gravitas and theological reference. Some apologists call this history 'scripturalised' and insist that there is a truth to the claims even if the truth isn't one of factual events and chronology, but one of theological truth (see John R. Hinnells in *The Routledge Companion to the Study of Religion*, 2010, p.403-5). However, the problem here is that in order to have some kind of symbolic truth to an account, one has to have some nugget, some element, of actual truth to the account upon which to hang the symbolic truth. If we go back to the genealogies of Jesus and agree with Foster that there is some kind of truth to the claim that Jesus was of Davidic heritage, that he was special; if we are to believe that which Matthew or Luke says about the heritage of Jesus; then there must be at least *some* truth to this. The point is that these two genealogies

---

[1] As we will see later, this is a technique used by Jewish rabbis to reinterpret meaning in older narratives in new and contemporarily relevant ways.

are the only *evidence* of this. Thus to insist that he *is* of Davidic lineage, but the only evidence that one provides is symbolic and not factual, seriously raises the question as to whether he actually *was* of Davidic lineage. If there is no nugget of truth underlying the symbolic claims, then the symbolic claims are meaningless.

In the example of the magi and Herod, if the events are supposed to fulfil a theological or symbolic objective, then there must be some truth underlying this to which the symbolism refers. But here it seems that every verse referring to the magi or Herod is fraught with issues. There simply is *no* truth underlying this potentially symbolic overlay other than, possibly, the assertion that 'Jesus is special'. Therefore, the claim that there is a symbolic truth to these accounts, or some other truth, is simply misplaced. Either there is some veracity to Jesus' heritage, to the magi and Herod interacting over the birth of Jesus, or there isn't. If there is, then where is it? As such, we have no basis for any belief that some magi or Herod were involved with the birth of Jesus and with that, we are left wondering exactly what must be learnt from the whole account. As John R. Hinnells in *The Routledge Companion to the Study of Religion* (2010, p. 403) illustrates:

> This tendency to find in the scripture whatever the community needs for its continuing development is remarkably widespread. This is in effect the purpose of all forms of figurative or non-literal interpretation, namely to enable the community to find there what it must. In many traditions this approach has been taken to considerable lengths, often through elaborate theories of multiple senses of scripture. In Christianity, there were sometimes as many as seven, but most often four: the literal, the allegorical, the moral and the anagogic (or relating to the end times).

None of which helps the case for the factual understanding of the events of the nativity, or in this case the magi and Herod. If it is a non-literal understanding, then it is for the development of the Christian tradition without regard for whether it is true or not. "Whatever the community need" is really what these accounts are about, and not "whatever might be true". Thus the "whatever the community need" becomes a sort of arbitrary guideline as to what is included in such scriptures, and has detrimental effect as to whether they might have any kind of historical or even theological verisimilitude.

With regard to the reflection of Daniel, it could be that God made these events transpire in such a way that one reflected another, but that both were historically veracious. On the other hand, it could just be that Matthew was trying to give the person of Jesus a theological deference and a biography that was not accurate by elevating him above the Old Testament prophets and kings through having him piggy-back on the events of the Old Testament. This reflective symmetry is, in this case, not an accurate account of events, but either an evolution of theology and biography that was originally very different, or an outright falsehood. Thus it is a case of probability. What is the most likely reason for the fact that there is a much later account of a potentially disputed man-god which entirely reflects an earlier account of a biblical great?

Let us begin to conclude this section by returning to Richard Carrier. Carrier continues, now exposing further comparative features with regard to the magi (Carrier 2006):

> In both texts (Matthew and the Septuagint text of Daniel) the stories have in their beginning the verb "to seal" (*sphragizô*), and in their endings the noun "eon" (*aiôn*, Daniel says "Oh king, live through all ages," Darius decrees "He is the living God through all ages," Jesus says "I am with you through all days until the end of the age"). Furthermore, in earliest Christian art, Daniel was the hero with whom Jesus was most commonly equated (cf. Thomas Matthews, *The Clash of the Gods*, 1993, pp. 77ff.), and Matthew alone depicts Magi visiting Christ at birth, whereas in the whole of the Old Testament the actual term "Magi" only appears in Daniel--for Daniel was most commonly associated with miracle working in the East. Since Matthew is clearly creating the guard story to create a seal and thus link Jesus with Daniel in death as in birth, the story is even less likely genuine than I grant above... The guard-placing account also
>
> involves the Sanhedrin both holding a meeting and placing a seal on a tombstone on the Sabbath, which is

strictly prohibited by Jewish law. Thus, Matthew shows them violating the Sabbath to work *against* the good, after having shown them attacking Jesus for violating the Sabbath to *do* good (12:1-14). So Matthew may be deliberately crafting a story to create a symbolic contrast, another reason we cannot be sure it is true.

This motif of sealing is the common thread between the two biblical narratives, according to Carrier. The magi both refuse to bend to the will of the insecure ruler and fulfil God's will. In an online essay / blog post (*The Luxor Thing*), Carrier affirms the following[1]:

> In the Daniel narrative, kings are troubled by omens and summon their wise men to explain them, including the magi and a foreigner, a Jew named Daniel (whom Christians regarded as among their principal prophets ...). In Matthew, a king is again troubled by an omen and summons his wise men to explain it, including the magi, who this time are the foreigners, and (in reversal of type) are the ones who get the omen right, and have come, in obedience to the decree of their ancestral king (Darius the Great, or so we're to believe), to worship the one true God, as all nations ought, thus fulfilling Daniel's message in Dan. 6:25-28, thus confirming Jesus is the Son of God, the very same God who rescued Daniel from the lions (and who will thus rescue Jesus).

As a result, I would posit that the magi are indeed a mechanism with which Matthew can bring in Herod in order to satisfy a theological objective of reflecting Moses' flight from Egypt, as I will later point out. Without the magi, there is no Herod. Furthermore, the magi provide another mechanism with which he can compare and liken Jesus to the much favoured Daniel to give Jesus (to a Jewish audience) a lofty position (in other words, better, even, than Daniel). This is prevalent since we also know of

---

[1]Richard Carrier, "The Luxor Thing", Feb 20 2012,
http://freethoughtblogs.com/carrier/archives/294 (retrieved 04/03/2012)

his Davidic heritage. In the eyes of the (Christian) Jews, then, Jesus is the greatest man imaginable. Jesus is, in fact, God.

13 – An unlikely Herod acts particularly na-ïvely

One has to wonder why, if travelling from the East, the star does not lead the magi directly to Bethlehem but to Jerusalem and then to Bethlehem. What becomes even more implausible is that Herod decided not to follow the star himself, but to task the itinerant wise men with going themselves and returning to him with the knowledge of Jesus' whereabouts. As Raymond Brown says (1977, p.190):

> Herod's failure to find the child at Bethlehem would be perfectly intelligible in a story in which there were no magi who came from the East and where he had only general scriptural knowledge about Bethlehem to guide him. It becomes ludicrous when the way to the house has been pointed out by a star which came to rest over it, and when the path to the door of the house in a small village has been blazed by exotic foreigners.

Given this, then, let us look at whether it is likely that the magi and the star were historical realities or whether they were agents used by the author for particular ends.

As we have seen from the previous section, Herod calls the magi to his palace in Jerusalem after hearing of them asking about the new king. This arouses his suspicions and he calls together his chief priests to tell him of the birth of the Messiah and where it should take place. If this really was an important Messianic prophecy, rather than a verse dug out of the Old Testament retrospectively, one would imagine that Herod and the general public would have been well aware that a Messiah was due to be born in the vicinity of Bethlehem at some point. The real estate prices in Bethlehem would be consistently extravagant. What is even more implausible is verse 3 in Matthew 2 which states that "When Herod the king heard this, he was troubled, and all Jerusalem with him." So the whole of Jerusalem knew of the birth of the Messiah. If this really was the case, the whole of the history of Judaism would have shifted from that point on; there would have been Jewish historical references to this great event. Jesus would have been properly heralded as the Messiah *if* all of Jerusalem knew of the birth of Jesus as a fulfilment of the prophecy from Micah. There is much that is strange and unbelievable about this whole episode. As Callahan (2002, p. 379) says:

> That king also acts strangely. Rather than counting on the wise men to tell him where the new king is to be found, why wouldn't he give them an escort or have them followed, or even have his own soldiers follow the star that is so visible to the wise men? In fact, there are two reasons for stopping at Herod's court, both having to do with establishing Jesus as the successor to the Davidic kings. The first of these is so the chief priests and scribes can announce that the scriptures say that the divine child will be born in Bethlehem. The second is so that Herod can know that the child is there, but not know exactly where in Bethlehem he is.

So Callahan points out the rather bizarre behaviour of the king in relying on some magi, whom he does not know from Adam, to return to him and act as seasoned spies, betraying the very person whom they have travelled no doubt for many hundreds of miles and many weeks to see! This is the hope of a very naïve man. Any betting person would tell you that he has slim to no chance of seeing those wise men again. You don't travel half of the known world to find and praise a new Messiah only to betray him *immediately*! Any decent king worth their salt would not exhibit such behaviour. Moreover, with a track record as vicious as Herod's, you would expect him to send a detachment with the wise men or to put them under some kind of arrest so that they could 'help him with his inquiries'. In addition, the time it would take the magi to go to Bethlehem and come back to Jerusalem there would be no guarantee, when the magi returned to Jerusalem and let Herod know of Jesus' exact whereabouts, that Joseph and family would still be in Bethlehem to be found by a returning Herod and entourage. As Strauss (1860, p. 160) agrees:

> On all these grounds, Herod's only prudent measure would have been either to detain the magi in Jerusalem, in the meantime by means of secret emissaries to dispatch the

child to whom such peculiar hopes were attached, and who must have been easy of discovery in the little village of Bethlehem ; or to have given the magi companions who, so soon as the child was found, might at once have put an end to his existence.

What Callahan, in the previous quote, also illustrates is that the magi *had* to stop off in Jerusalem in order to give Matthew a mechanism to bring Herod into the story as well as a mechanism to allow Herod to have heard of this birth. Without the magi turning up and shouting around Jerusalem "Has anyone seen the new Messiah?" (itself an unlikely thing) and alerting Herod, we would have had no Herod, no massacring of the babies and no reason for Joseph and family to flee to Egypt. This fleeing to Egypt is a crucial event, thematically speaking, for Matthew's account as we shall learn later seems rather dependent on a highly implausible contrivance dictated by Matthew himself.

There is another fundamental problem with the behaviour of Herod as is so well set out by Strauss (1860, p. 159). In Matthew 2: 7-8, we have the following announcement: "Then Herod secretly called the magi and determined from them the exact time the star appeared. And he sent them to Bethlehem..." So before sending the magi to Bethlehem he is finding out the position of the star for an as yet unknown reason. But verse 16 indicates a reason as Herod "sent and slew all the male children who were in Bethlehem and all its vicinity, from two years old and under, according to the time which he had determined from the magi." Yet how can this have happened with this chronology? As Strauss (1860, p.159) says:

> But this plan of murdering all the children of Bethlehem up to a certain age... was not conceived by Herod until after the magi had disappointed his expectation that they would return to Jerusalem : a deception which, if we may judge from his violent anger on account of it Herod had by no means anticipated. Prior to this ... it had been his intention to obtain from the magi, on their return, so great a description of the child, his dwelling and circumstances, that it would be easy for him to remove his infantine rival without sacrificing any other life.

So it wasn't until after he had discovered that the magi had not returned to him that he had to change his actions and seek to put to death all infants under the age of two. He was pretty damned lucky, then, to have "ascertained this time before he had decided on the plan". Asking the magi about the star was only relevant if and only if they were not to return to him, if they deceived him. As Strauss points out, his anger shows he was not expecting this and gets away with being able to calculate such a morbid ruling because he had somehow asked them for the relevant information before he needed it! Matthew's chronology is woeful here and this makes the account even more contrived.

So yet again we have a set of events which seem incredibly unrealistic and unlikely, and which are incredibly artificially manufactured in order to allow for certain other events to unfold. In this way, the magi are nothing more than a literary and theological mechanism employed by the writer with little or no likelihood of being factually true.

14 – The star was not a real and natural star

I find it hard to comprehend why conservative and fundamentalist Christians, who believe the Bible's miracles to be actual events, would even try to find natural explanations for what the Bible clearly describes as divine supernatural phenomena. The Jehovah of the Scriptures has awesome powers to suspend natural laws and do whatever He wants. Why trouble to look for natural causes of the great downpour by which God drowned every man, woman, and child on Earth, as well as their pets, except for one undistinguished family and the few animals they took on their Ark?[1]

The story of the magi has a lot to answer for, not least because the three wise men were supposed to have followed a star from the East to their destination at a Bethlehem stable. This star has caused a huge amount of consternation over the years. One could straight away ask whether it was an astronomical event, or something supernaturally divined. In many translations of the Bible (e.g. the New International Version), the star is claimed to have risen, thus inferring a heliacal rising. This is when a star rises from the eastern horizon after it has not been visible for some time. And this presents the first problem. The star seems to have been moving in the wrong direction for it to have been a naturalistic phenomenon. As Phil Plait in a 2007 article in *The Discover Magazine* maintains:

So if the wise men saw a star "in the east", we see immediately there are problems. Was it in the east at sunset? If so, it would rise until about midnight, whereupon it would be toward the south, and then by sunrise it would be in the west. Following it would make them go in circles. Because of the Earth's rotation, a star cannot stay in the eastern part of the sky. If it's in the east at sunrise that's

---

[1] Martin Gardner in his article "The Star of Bethlehem", *The Skeptical Inquirer*

111

both better and worse; better because the star may still be in the east when the Sun rises, so they *only* see it toward the east, but worse because then how can they then follow it?

It's not an option for the star to be only in the east all night long. The rotating Earth prevents that. And if it's far enough north it can stay in the north, but that's not what the Bible says. It's very specific about it being in the east; Matthew states that not just once but twice.

There are only two options: if it stayed in the east then it either orbited the Earth at a nearly or exactly geo-synchronous rate (taking 24 hours to go around once, so it appeared to hang in one spot in the sky like a TV satellite), or it was a miracle and just hung there. The first is physi-cally impossible, and the second... well, if you assume it was a miracle, why look for a supportive scientific explana-tion at all?

It does make you wonder why many apologists seek to find a naturalistic explanation for something which is so clearly super-naturalistic, and it seems to open up apologists to more issues than it solves.

As far as it being a naturalistic phenomenon, there have been many apologists who have sought to reconcile the event with astrological movements in and around the suspected time of Jesus' birth. As Raymond Brown says (1977, p.170), there was "popular opinion that each person has a star which begins to give light when he is born and fades out when he dies". One important point to make here is that in contemporary literature (now seen as mythology) stars were seen as accompanying premonitory indica-tions to births; that the people whose births were accompanied by such symbolic stars would go on to be great people. Thus, as Brown continues, "Matthew's age would not have found bizarre the claim that a star rose to herald the birth of the King of the Jews and subsequently guided magi-astrologers in their quest to find him." Other literary examples of such a practise include Virgil who guided Aeneas to Rome with a star; Alexander the Great, whose supremacy was predicted with a star at his birth; Abraham, who was heralded with bright constellation at his birth according to Jewish literature; Augustus; Alexander Severus; Mithradates of Pontus and many more to boot. Tacitus (*Annals* 14:22) suggested that there was a general belief that a comet meant a change of emperor was imminent. As early Christian scholar Eusebius claimed:

> In the case of other remarkable and famous men we know that strange stars have appeared, what some call *comets*, or *meteors*, or *tails of fire*, or similar phenomena that are seen in connection with great unusual events. But what event could be greater or more important for the whole Universe than the spiritual light coming to all (b) men through the Saviour's Advent, bringing to human souls the gift of holiness and true knowledge of God? Wherefore the herald star gave the great sign, telling in symbol that the Christ of God would shine as a great new light on all the world.
>
> And the prophecy foretells a man as well as a star, for it says: "A star shall rise out of Jacob, and a man shall spring from Israel,"...[1]

The prophecy he is referring to is Numbers 24:17: "A star shall come forth from Jacob, A sceptre shall rise from Israel, And shall crush through the forehead of Moab, And tear down all the sons of Sheth." We can see, therefore, that it was generally accepted, expected perhaps, that great people were heralded by astronomical phenomena. If Jesus was to not only compete but surpass the importance of such great people then one could only expect a similar treatment. As to whether it happened at all, let us look further into the machinations of the heavens.

Over the centuries, many attempts have been made to find stellar conjunctions or novae which correlate with the star of Bethlehem, without any lasting success.

One such claim is that there was, in 7 or 6 BCE, a triple conjunction of Jupiter and Saturn. This has often, starting with Johannes Kepler, been cited as the Star of Bethlehem. However, according to contemporary Babylonian astronomical sources, there was nothing of any such importance in the skies at this time:

---

[1] *Demonstratio Evangelica*, Book 9, Chapter 1

In fact, one of the Babylonian tablets in the British Museum is an astronomical almanac for the years 7/6 BC, which covers the period of the triple conjunction which is a widely commented candidate to have been the Star of Bethlehem. The almanac explicitly speaks of the movements of the two planets. The tablet, catalogued as BM 35429, makes neither direct reference, nor allusion to the conjunction.

... As can be seen from the above extracts [a translation of the tablets], the conjunction seems to have given rise to no perceptible comment or interest, either in the triple conjunction ... or in the planetary massing. If the Magi were Babylonian astronomers it seems odd that, if this event was the Star of Bethlehem, they made no comment that indicates any interest in it at all.[1]

Some, such as astronomer Karlis Kaufmanis, claim[2] that the star was indeed the conjunction, and that the fact there was a triple conjunction allows for the fact that the star seems to have disappeared when the magi visited Herod and reappeared afterward to settle on Bethlehem. As Martin Gardner (1999) points out in his "The Star of Bethlehem", though:

Kepler later had doubts about his conjecture. As astronomer Roy K. Marshall points out in his booklet *The Star of Bethlehem* ... Jupiter and Saturn, throughout the period of their proximity, were never closer together than two diameters of the Moon as it appears in the sky. In 1846 British astronomer Charles Pritchard did some careful research on the event. Because of the erratic looping paths of the two planets, as seen from Earth, there were three separate close encounters. Astronomers call it a "triple conjunction."

The two giant planets were closest on May 29, October 1, and December 5. "Even with . . . the strange postulate of someone with weak eyes," Pritchard wrote, "the planets

---

[1] "Chinese and Babylonian Observations"
(http://www.astrosurf.com/comets/Star_of_Bethlehem/English/Chinese.htm retrieved 10/02/2012)
[2] "The Star of Bethlehem", Karlis Kaufmanis
(http://www.astro.umn.edu/news/vol18.pdf retrieved 10/02/2012)

could not have appeared as one star." Marshall adds: "Only an abysmally weak pair of eyes could have ever merged them."

So it doesn't look good for the triple conjunction theory which is generally seen as weak anyway. The magi, by rights, should have been much more excited some sixty years earlier when the same conjunction was much closer (in 66 BCE). Moreover, as is not really mentioned by the likes of Kaufmanis, each of these conjunctions lasted only a few days, clearly not long enough for the magi to be guided on their huge journey from the East. The planets also would have undergone rising and setting like any other star, and this is clearly not what Matthew implies by a lingering star.

Another suggestion is that the star was some sort of comet. A comet is a less likely explanation due to the fact that they were seen in these times as being a *bad* omen, not a good one heralding the birth of the Messiah. Comets are also not particularly easy to confuse with stars, especially since the magi would have been astronomers (as mentioned, this is often the translation of magi, wise men or astrologers / astronomers). There are no decent candidates for comets[1], either, which lie within the timeframe needed to correlate with the birth of Jesus. The only possible reference to what *might* have been a comet lies in Chinese records of observations in around 5 BCE. However, this is problematic:

> A theory which has been popular for many years is that the Star of Bethlehem was a comet. There is no doubt that a bright comet is a very spectacular event and would be an impressive "star", but scrutiny of the Chinese and Babylonian chronicles reveals no evidence of a bright comet. There is an event observed in 5 BC which may be an account of a comet, but there is no description of classical elements in Chinese reports such as the tail and the comet's movement which make it doubtful that this was a comet. Similarly, the Chinese reports imply that the object was sta-

---

[1] As Joe Rao (2011) says, "…it seems unlikely that another Great Comet could have appeared nearer to the accepted time frame of the Star's appearance and went unrecorded".

tionary — most uncometary in an object seen for two and a half months.[1]

The Journal of the British Astronomy Association itself concludes (Jenkins 2004, p. 338), "This lack of an agreed interpretation in itself points to the conclusion that the Star of Bethlehem was not an actual astronomical event." In fact, the author suggests that Matthew may well have seen the comet of 66 CE which would have given him something to think about when constructing his own account. Not only that, but, as Jenkins continues:

> In addition, during these times it is a historical fact that a deputation of Magi *did* come from the east to bring gifts and pay homage, and they *did* return home by another route. Also a bright comet with an impressive tail appeared over Jerusalem.
>
> In AD 66 Tiridates, the King of Armenia, led a notable procession of Magi to pay homage to Nero. After Nero had confirmed Tiridates as the King of Armenia 'the King did not return by the route he had followed in coming', but sailed back to Armenia by a different route. He came through Illyricum and north of the Ionian Sea and returned by sailing from Brundisium to Dyrrachium.

This was Halley's Comet which appeared brightly over Jerusalem and which was potentially a portent for the Jewish-Roman War and the destruction of the Temple in Jerusalem in 70 CE. Jenkins argues that Matthew was probably using this comet as a basis for the Star of Bethlehem and the arrival of the magi from the East. This does appear to be a very good hypothesis indeed. From the evidence we have, it appears wholly unlikely that a comet was actually witnessed at the time of Jesus' birth, and certainly not in the manner described. At the end of the day, a comet is not a star.

---

[1] Possible Explanations of the Star of Bethlehem (http://www.observadores-cometas.com/cometas/Star/Possible.html retrieved 10/02/2012)

The third option for a naturalistic explanation of events would be a nova or supernova (an extremely luminous stellar explosion). Again we have similar issues. Such bright occurrences should be well attested, but as Brown says (1977, p. 171) "There is no record of a nova or supernova just before Jesus' birthdate". He, himself, proclaims a conjunction as the most likely candidate, but that falls well short of being likely.

Brown (1977, p. 172) points out that such astronomical occurrences may not have been historical bases for Matthew's account of the star, but acted more as reinterpretation by association with the birth of Jesus. And yet, as Foster (2007, p.69) concludes about the whole matter of the star:

> But none of these [naturalistic astronomical phenomena] tallies well with Matthew. No known heavenly body could have gone ahead of the magi, leading them to Bethlehem. None of them could have stopped over the place where a boy was born. And Matthew knew it. He was describing a miracle.

It is refreshing to hear so rational a Christian voice on the topic. So where does this leave us? Well, with the claim that it was (simply) a miracle, that there was no corresponding astronomical sight which guided the magi to their destination. The star was a supernatural event. And I would urge you to reread Gardner's quote at the beginning of this section.

Such reliance on the notion that the star was indeed a visible entity, but that it was supernatural in ontology, is itself fraught with issues. If, indeed, the magi did follow the star from the East and from Jerusalem to Bethlehem then it is entirely conspicuous that no other witness reported such an incredible and miraculous occurrence. This was a bright and highly unusual event that must have warranted many witnesses and ensuing reports or accounts. We simply have no extra-biblical accounts of either a natural or supernatural astronomical event which matches the behaviour or description or chronology of the Matthean narrative. On top of this, we have a problem with an account of a star that can rest over a house. A single house could not be pointed out by a star unless it came down from the sky and literally rested over the house. This is, of course, possible with an omnipotent God. However, the whole of Bethlehem would have been out of their houses marvelling at the wonder of such an event. And this would not have gone unreported, I wager.

Perhaps the star was only visible to the magi. If this was the case, then the prophecy is very narrow and only applicable to the magi, and Herod would have been calculating the timing of a astronomical body which only existed in their minds. This explanation will not suffice (aside from ostensibly allowing anything ad hoc and untestable to be claimed, invalidating any need for, or ability for there to be, corroborating evidence. Perhaps everything in these accounts only happened in the minds of the protagonists, but this is ridiculous and unfalsifiable).

The only plausible explanation is that this was yet another mechanism employed by the Gospel writer for theological and literary ends, guiding our magi to Herod and ensuring that Herod kills the innocents and sends Jesus to Egypt, only to then be able to come "out of Egypt".

15 – The magi as Balaam reinterpreted

The Old Testament includes an oft-cited account, cited because of the many hallmarks it shares with Matthew's account of the magi following the star out of the East. The Numbers 24:17 quote mentioned earlier ("I see him, but not now; I behold him, but not near; A star shall come forth from Jacob, A sceptre shall rise from Israel") are the words uttered by Balaam. So who was Balaam, and how do his actions relate to the magi?

Balaam was a notorious prophet, in the Old Testament, from Mesopotamia. "Thus Balaam's reluctant, but divinely inspired, prophecy"[1], it is claimed, stated that a future king would be accompanied by a star. Balaam was a seer summoned by the then Transjordanian King of Moab, Balak. Balak feared the Israelites, who were being led out of Egypt by Moses. There are definitely parallels between the Pharaoh and Balak and Herod, which is itself potentially important to the Matthean narrative. So Balak finds need for this *magos* Balaam, an enchanter and visionary (Brown 1977, p. 193). Balaam ends up being slain by the Israelites but some good comes out of this ostensibly unsavoury character in the form of the prophecy. Just to make things easier, let me list the similarities between the two accounts:

- Balaam and the magi "came from the East"
- Balaam and the magi were all... magi. In fact, it is often claimed[2] that Balaam was the first, the founder, of the magi tradition.
- The magi were probably three and Balaam also came out of the East as three, with two servants (Numbers 22:22).
- Balaam foiled Balak by revealing oracles predicting the greatness of Israel and its royal ruler. The magi

---

[1] As Henry Morris states in "When They Saw the Star", for the Institute for Creation Research.
[2] E.g. Morris

foiled Herod, also revealing a great ruler over all of Israel.
- Herod and Balak are comparable kings.
- These despotic kings used foreign magi to rid themselves of an enemy but the magi end up honouring the enemies.
- The Pharaoh and his scribes conspire against Moses upon hearing of his birth as Herod and his scribes conspire against Jesus upon hearing of his birth.
- Dreams and visions are used in both stories.
- The prophecy of Balaam supposedly directly foretelling the Messiah (which was understood as such in pre-Jesus times, such as with the Qumran community[1]).
- After the main events of the story, "Balaam went off to his home" (Numbers 24:25) and the magi "went away to their own country" (Matthew 2:12).

Although Matthew had very clear objectives within the theological framework of his Gospel that would seek to retain observance of the Jewish law for Jews, gentiles also play an important role. There is an implicit understanding that the world would become one community of gentile and Jew under Jesus. Matthew shows that there is precedent in the Old Testament for God revealing important ideas of salvation to and through gentiles. As scholars W.D. Davies and Dale Allison[2] (2000, p.231) point out, "Matthew probably thought of the magi as 'Balaam's successors'".

The point for the intents and purposes of this section, though, is whether this makes the Matthean narrative of the magi more or less likely to be historically veracious. Does it follow that an account is false simply because it echoes or reflects an earlier account? Or that it uses an earlier account as a skeleton or vehicle

[1] Brown (1977) p.195
[2] For length of title, let me initially reference it here: *A Critical and Exegetical Commentary on the Gospel According to Saint Matthew: in Three Volumes. Introduction and Commentary on Matthew 1-VII, Volume 1*

to deliver its message? This is something I have touched upon earlier in this book and it depends upon what strategy you adopt for analysing the Bible. Since God, omnipotent and omniscient, is apparently capable of doing anything conceivable within the logical ranges of his characteristics, then it is clearly conceivable that he could give Balaam such a prophecy, and that he could order the world so that one story reflected another (supposedly 1400 years earlier) in so much detail so as to be theologically significant. Of course he could do this, but is it likely? Intuitively, I would think it as less likely that, for theological reasons, God would arrange the universe in such a manner. This is a point I touched upon in one of my earlier books, *Free Will?* (p. 209-210), in which I look at the implications of an earlier prophecy to a later event, this time with only a six hundred year gap:

> So for Jesus to be prophesied, God has to ensure that he has the right parents, who have to be, for prophetic rea-sons and reasons of Jewish authority, in the lineage of David. This is no small organisational feat—the family line must be kept alive throughout the years. In fact, the order is taller than you might think since it is often not a case of en-suring things *do* happen, but ensuring that things *don't* happen. Mary, for example, cannot be bitten by that poi-sonous snake when she was 12, must not have injured her uterus when the plough skewed into her abdomen at 14, must not have slipped off the wall she was walking along a week later, must not have starved due to a poverty stricken lifestyle, must not have been miscarried, must not have contracted an early form of cancer, must not have... the list is tremendous. And that is just for Mary in her short life. One has to map out the entire history of the world to ensure the rest. It has to be ensured that Jesus doesn't die in some way before his time of preaching and atonement. The entire ancestral line of his parents must be preserved... The Egyp-tians must not have been allowed to kill their Hebrew slaves, the surrounding empires must not have obliterated the Israelites in a major conquest, a volcanic eruption must not have wiped out the Middle East, a meteorite must not hit earth, man must have evolved in a certain way from the original life-form. So on, and so on, to the point that, in or-

121

der to ensure that Jesus would come down in the fashion predicted, some 600 years later, God has to micro-manage the entire universe, and this smacks, just a little, of determinism.

Without wanting to get into a side-issue of debating the implications of prophecy, one can see that they are, at least, highly problematic. It just seems somewhat far-fetched that God would arrange the world's history in such a way that there would be historical and theological symmetry in events separated by 1400 years.

So could Matthew be contriving his record of events in such a way that it mirrors the Balaam story but still contains nuggets of truth? Well, this is certainly possible. However, since we have looked at other evidence (the lack of historical support for a star, natural or otherwise; the bizarre accounting of events with regard to their and Herod's behaviours) and we will look at further evidence that calls their existence into doubt, one can say with good probability that the magi did not exist and did not carry out their reported actions. It does look like a case of all or nothing and the evidence and probability supports the case for nothing.

In order for Matthew's accounting to be correct, this is what is essentially happening:

- A supernatural star appears a huge distance from Bethlehem and leads (probably) three different magi on a massive journey to which or whom only they can guess.
- No one else sees this star, or at least nobody records its bizarre behaviour, in a very astrologically and astronomically astute time.
- The magi get sidetracked to Jerusalem.
- Herod acts entirely bizarrely.
- All of Jerusalem is reminded of a prophecy that they must have forgotten and gets disturbed, none of which is recorded anywhere else.
- The magi continue to follow this star which rests over a house, trusted entirely by a wicked and untrusting king.
- No one continues to see or report this star.

122

- The world (Jerusalem, the shepherds, the magi) forgets Jesus is the Messiah until he is killed around thirty years later.
- The magi and shepherds disappear never to be seen or heard from again. As we shall see in a later section, this is strange since they have travelled so far. One would have expected them to evangelise in their homeland, being influential people.
- Their story mirrors, with incredible parity, an earlier theologically relevant tale.

Thus, in order to take the account of the magi seriously and to believe it as historically accurate we must jump through these incredibly unbelievable and unlikely hoops.

I have had conversations with Christians who have claimed that you don't have to take a historical truth from such accounts, but that the truth can be symbolic, partial or theological. This I have touched on earlier, but allow me to go into further detail. It is customary in Jewish rabbinical tradition to interpret and reinterpret Holy Scripture. New meaning is extracted from older texts in a continual manner known as *midrash*. As theologian Robert Price in his essay "New Testament Narrative as Old Testament Midrash" states, "the stories comprising the Gospels and the Acts of the Apostles are themselves the result of haggadic midrash upon stories from the Old Testament". Bishop John Shelby Spong, a liberal Christian scholar, wrote a book looking predominantly at this very issue (*Liberating the Gospels: Reading the Bible with Jewish Eyes*). It seems that this kind of midrashic approach of rehashing the Old Testament within a New Testament framework does remove oneself from a literalist view of the Bible. As Spong says (1997, p. 325) it "might also help the searching and questioning Christian avoid the faithless despair that engulfs the person who feels that 'no' is the only honest answer to the question: 'Did it really happen?'" But what of a claimed symbolic or theological truth? It appears, to me at any rate, that a theological truth is meaningless without something or someone to apply it to; that this person must be real in order to allow the theology to have any purchase. Yet a few pages later (1997, p.332) Spong claims that Jesus is "for me the conduit through which the love of God was loosed into human history". But what *is* that history if everything one investigates turns out to be theological overlay? Who was this Jesus if one cannot fathom any nugget of truth in the biographical claims of Jesus made in the Gospels? If the intent was not to give true historical biography then where *is* the biography, the evidence that supports any claim of who Jesus was and in what manner he existed? To support a case for a historical Jesus, such historical truth must exist somewhere, and if it does not then we cannot at all be sure of whom Jesus is claimed to be by the Gospel writers or any subsequent writer.

In simple terms, without any historical or factual foundation, the edifice that is the historical and theological Jesus comes tumbling down. You can't build a reality on theological assertion alone, especially if it is second hand.

16 – Separating the sheep from the goats

Luke summons his own people to praise the newly born Messiah. Unimpressed or unaware of the exotic foreigners, the enchanters from the East, Luke is more down-to-earth, more blue-collar with his approach. Let us remind ourselves of the passage in Luke 2:8-20:

In the same region there were some shepherds staying out in the fields and keeping watch over their flock by night. And an angel of the Lord suddenly stood before them, and the glory of the Lord shone around them; and they were terribly frightened. But the angel said to them, "Do not be afraid; for behold, I bring you good news of great joy which will be for all the people; for today in the city of David there has been born for you a Savior, who is Christ the Lord. This will be a sign for you: you will find a baby wrapped in cloths and lying in a manger." And suddenly there appeared with the angel a multitude of the heavenly host praising God and saying,

"Glory to God in the highest, And on earth peace among men with whom He is pleased."

When the angels had gone away from them into heaven, the shepherds began saying to one another, "Let us go straight to Bethlehem then, and see this thing that has happened which the Lord has made known to us." So they came in a hurry and found their way to Mary and Joseph, and the baby as He lay in the manger. When they had seen this, they made known the statement which had been told them about this Child. And all who heard it wondered at the things which were told them by the shepherds. But Mary treasured all these things, pondering them in her heart. ²he shepherds went back, glorifying and praising God for all that they had heard and seen, just as had been told them.

Multitudes of angels are an awe-inspiring sight, no doubt, but one can understand if there were no corroborating witnesses to such a sight in the middle of the countryside. However, what becomes a little less realistic is the idea that the shepherds "went back, glorifying and praising God for all that they had heard and seen, just as had been told them." The problem here is that it is claimed that the shepherds (some shepherds means that we have little idea of how many) returned home praising God for everything they had seen and yet we hear nothing of the shepherds again and we only hear about Jesus' Messianic characteristics some thirty years later. There are simply no other claims about such a birth and about such a person until Paul and the Gospels. It all comes as such a massive surprise to the Jews of Israel, and yet we know that the shepherds would have been telling everyone about their incredible experience until they died. Furthermore, we know that "all who heard" refers to an audience of people present when the shepherds arrived. Who were these people, and why do they not spread the wonderful news of the Messiah? This would have been a life-changing moment of amazing magnitude and yet no one else knows of the experience of these shepherds. Is this better explained by the notion that it really happened as set out by Luke, or is it better explained by the notion that these shepherds were merely symbolic and theological devices? I am of the opinion that these sorts of difficult-to-rationalise situations are better explained by the latter.

Firstly, let me point out that there have been some arguments over the years focusing on the fact that if the nativity did take place in winter time that the shepherds would not have been out with their flocks. However, I am not too worried over exactly when during the year this happened since there is, to me, little indication other than tradition as to exactly when the birth took place.

Whilst shepherds were generally looked down upon by the majority of Jews of the era, Luke was seen to be writing in a Greco-Roman tradition where shepherds were held in high regard. As New Testament scholar Helmut Köster, says in *Ancient Christian Gospels: their History and Development* (1990, p. 308):

But even the proclamation to the shepherds about the child in the manger appeals to general beliefs of the Greco-Roman world. In the Jewish tradition at the time of Jesus, shepherds are not generally seen in a very positive light. But in Greco-Roman mythology, legend, and poetry the shepherd represents the golden age at which gods and human beings live in harmony and nature is at peace.

This, as Köster states, is in contrast to Matthew's approach as he creates his narrative in "a very biblical environment" (p. 307). Again, we are beginning to see the shepherds, as with the Matthean use of the magi, as mechanisms rather than incidental characters in a historical account. I have often thought that between the two accounts, Matthew and Luke, we see Jesus as the Messiah appealing to the rich and influential (represented by the magi) and to the poor and lowly (represented by the shepherds[1]). In this way, the Messiah speaks for and to the whole spectrum of humanity, gentile and Jew alike. This is reflected in Mary's Magnificat, Luke 1:52, uttered by Mary prior to the birth narrative: "He has brought down rulers from their thrones, And has exalted those who were humble." We must also remember that David, of Bethlehem, was a shepherd, something which would not have gone unnoticed to the Jewish reader.

Brown (1977, p. 420-4) also shows how Luke is using, in a midrashic manner, writings in Micah to show a connection between the pasturing shepherds and the Old Testament. Brown tells us that sheep from between Midgal Eder (Tower of the Flock near Bethlehem) and Jerusalem were used for the highly religiously important Temple sacrifices.

Such derivation from Old Testament sources is maintained by D.F. Strauss who claims that both Gospels are derived independently from Old Testament sources, implying that historical veracity was not top of the list of concerns for either writer (1860, p. 176):

> This derivation is too elaborate to be probable, even were it true... that Luke's narrative bears the stamp of historical credibility. As, however, we conceive that we have

---

[1] See Joel Green in *The Gospel of Luke*, p. 130.

127

proved the contrary, and as, consequently, we have before us two equally unhistorical narratives ... traced through Old Testament passages and Jewish notions... [They are] two variations on the same theme, composed, however, quite independently of each other.

So what are we left with? The shepherds, as mentioned, seem to be a little contrived to register as a historically veracious set of characters. An absence of evidence is indeed an issue when appraising whether such an account is historically reliable or not. As we shall investigate later, when there are claims of so many involved in a narrative who are unheard of again and who seemingly tell no one else of such amazing things, then we must be somewhat suspicious of whether they are claims of historical veracity.

17 – Herod's Massacre of the Innocents as uncorroborated and symbolic

Herod was a nasty piece of work, of that we are sure. On realising that the magi were not going to return with that vital information concerning the whereabouts of a newborn outsider in a small village, Herod decided to take it upon himself to use the fortunately gathered information of the location of the star in the sky and calculate the maximum age that Jesus could have been. With this information he ordered the murder of all the children under two in and around Bethlehem. There is much to investigate over this claim of Matthew's.

Firstly, let us look at how many children would have died and whether this would be something that would be planned by an all-loving God. The number of children is hotly debated— Christians look to minimise the number by claiming the village was small (which doesn't help their case for Herod not simply marching in and looking for the newborn baby) whilst critics often seek to aggrandise the number. The number of dead has, historically, been estimated to be as much as 144,000 (from Coptic sources as mentioned in the Catholic Encyclopedia[1]) which is clearly ridiculous. The Catholic Encyclopedia continues:

> This cruel deed of Herod is not mentioned by the Jewish historian Flavius Josephus, although he relates quite a number of atrocities committed by the king during the last years of his reign. The number of these children was so small that this crime appeared insignificant amongst the other misdeeds of Herod.

The same source uses further sources to argue that the deaths number as few as twenty or even six. Of course, since we don't know how far "the vicinity" of Bethlehem stretched, it is hard to be so sure that the number would be so few. We have little idea of the size of the "City of Bethlehem" and how large its vicin-

---

[1] Holy Innocents, The Catholic Encyclopedia,
http://ww.newadvent.org/cathen/07419a.htm (retrieved 16/02/2012)

ity was. To claim only six died seems to be stretching plausibility given that it happened at all. And given that it is called a massacre, we might assume a few more perished. William Albright and C.S. Mann estimate that at the time of Jesus' birth the population of Bethlehem was about 600, meaning that there would have been around six children of the correct age and gender (*The Anchor Bible. Matthew,* Albright and Mann, 1971, p. 19). However, even if this claim by the biblical literalist Albright is true, it seems not to have taken into account that the population had swollen (there was no room for Joseph and his family) if we can believe that Joseph and his partner had themselves ventured there to have a baby. How many other outsiders were there with young children? Remember, if Joseph at forty-one generations into his past was seeking to come to Bethlehem for the census, then how many others from the whole province (or even from other provinces) were also doing likewise?

Peter Richardson, in his book *Herod: King of the Jews and Friend of the Romans* (1999, p. 297) states "there is little in the story that carries historical conviction". Brown (1977, p.227), as an eminent Catholic scholar, agrees in saying "There are serious reasons for thinking that the Flight to Egypt and the massacre at Bethlehem may not be historical". As far as the numbers are concerned, figures at the lower end would obviously better support historical credibility.

Though the numbers may have been smaller than at first interpreted, the crime is still an atrocious one. It certainly fits in with the character of Herod who committed some pretty tasteless atrocities. However, these were very well documented, especially towards the end of his life, by the likes of Josephus. Even if the numbers had been as low as twenty, this still amounts to a form of genocide in an area in his own back yard. Such a ruthless and callous crime would still warrant mention. Josephus mentions an awful lot yet there is absolutely no reference whatsoever to such a task. This is all the more unbelievable when given the reason for doing this. It is not so much the action but the reason for carrying it out which is so noteworthy. I really do believe that apologists who defend this absence of evidence are pushing the boundaries of plausibility. It is not just that the king of a province took it upon himself to kill a number of male babies under the age of two who were all his own subjects, but the fact that all of Jerusalem seemed to be aware of this, or at least of the fact that he was very angry that the Messiah, the new King of the Jews, had been born. There seems to be a lack of joined-up thinking on show when apologists simply refuse to acknowledge such a glaring absence of any corroborating evidence for this whole episode. It's simply not a numbers game, but a king doing a very public and atrocious thing due to a very publicly known prophecy fulfilment with exotic magi alerting an entire city and their priests and scribes, and said king being exceptionally angry. Quite why none of this is reported can only lead one to conclude that it most probably did not happen. As David Fitzgerald, in *Nailed* (2010, p. 23-24) states:

> It beggars belief to think anyone would have missed an outrage as big as the massacre of every infant boy in the area around a town just 6 miles from Jerusalem—and yet there is no corroboration for it in any account, Jewish, Greek or Roman. It's not even found in any of the other Gospels—only Matthew's.

If we add this (lack of) evidence together with the fact that Luke singularly neglects to mention the entire episode as well, then the case for historical credibility looks even shakier.

So if it likely did not happen, then why has it ended up in the Gospel of Matthew? Well, one prominent theory is, as Richardson (1999, p.288) points out, "It seems likely that Herod's killing of his own children prompted the report of his murder of a larger group of children." One of Herod's most famous (though now superseded by the notoriety of the slaughter of the innocents) misdemeanours was the killing of his own wife and sons. As Josephus says (*Antiquities* 15.7.4,5):

> His passion also made him stark mad and leaping out of his bed he ran around the palace in a wild manner. His sister Salome took the opportunity also to slander Miriam and to confirm his suspicions about Joseph [Miriam's alleged lover]. Then out of his ungovernable jealousy and rage he commanded both of them to be killed immediately. But as soon as his passion was over he repented of what he had done and as soon as his anger was

> worn off his affections were kindled again ... Indeed, the
> flame of his desires for her was so hard that he could not
> think she was dead but he would appear under his disor-
> ders to speak to her as if she were still alive...

Herod had some ten marriages; he had three of his sons put to death, so horrible things were not beyond him. Is it, as Richardson says, that the very real story of Herod killing his own children is an inspiration for the story of the massacre of the innocents? Perhaps it provided Matthew with the perfect vehicle with which he could deliver prophecy and the Moses narrative.

Now that we can see that Matthew might have had the seed of an idea to work with here, let us look at the Moses account to see the comparative similarities. In the Old Testament book of Exodus, we hear the account of Moses asking the Pharaoh of Egypt if he could let his enslaved people go. Moses, in a position of some responsibility, is told no. In the end, Moses is allowed to go, but the Pharaoh changes his mind and chases him. At the Red Sea (or Sea of Reeds, depending on how it is translated), Moses leads his Hebrew followers across an area that has been parted. The Pharaoh's men, on the other hand, are caught in the waters and killed. For some forty years, the Hebrews wonder around the desert (probably the area of Kadesh-Barnea) until they wonder themselves out into Canaan. The Hebrews are led out of Egypt by Moses in a journey involving huge amounts of faith in God. I will talk about the flight from and to Egypt in the next section. I want to concentrate, here, on the events that inspired the Passover celebrations.

When the Pharaoh was refusing to let the Israelite slaves go, God sent the ten plagues to Egypt in order to bend his arm. The last of the plagues was the death of all the first-born Egyptians. The Israelites, in order to alert the murderous angels to their own innocent whereabouts, marked their doorposts with lambs' blood. The angels passed over the Israelites domiciles to kill the Egyptian first-borns. This truly *was* a massacre of innocents. If the whole of Egypt was given this treatment, then the numbers of murdered children would have been truly staggering, and for no crime, it seems, other than being born into a country whose ruler was the Pharaoh.

As far as the Herodian act is concerned, some arguments seek to defend a historical position. Macrobius, writing some 400 years later, wrote of a quote from the Emperor Augustus. As E.G. Sihler states in *The New Sclaff-Herzog Encyclopedia of Religious Knowledge*[1]:

> In the Saturnalia (II., 4, 11) of Macrobius, the Roman writer in the fifth century, is this anecdote: "When he (Augustus) heard that among the boys whom in Syria Herod, the king of the Jews, had ordered to be killed there were infants of two years and under, he exclaimed: 'I had rather be a pig of Herod's than a son.'" As the Saturnalia contains many anecdotes which carry with them indubitable evidence of being of contemporary origin, there is no reason for supposing that this one was the creation of a time subsequent to Augustus, but every probability that it, too, was contemporary, and so is an incidental, undesigned, but striking witness to the truthfulness of the Gospel story.

The problem with using Macrobius is that he has overlaid the original quote from Augustus with reference to the Massacre of the Innocents rather than what is thought to be the original subject, Herod's murder of his own children (see Brown 1977, p. 226). The quote relies on a pun comparing Herod's brutality to his own son with the notion that he wouldn't eat pork. Macrobius appears to be supplying a setting to the quote, based on his own contemporary, albeit pagan but contextually Christian, reading. Brown also concludes that it is likely that "the setting in Macrobius has been influenced by the story in Matthew" (1977, p. 226).

So, importantly, the key here, as Brown (1977, p. 228) also claims, is that:

> Matthew did not draw upon an account of historical events but rewrote a pre-Matthean narrative associating the birth of Jesus, son of Joseph, with the patriarch Joseph and the birth of Moses.

---

[1] Vol. VI: Innocents – Liudger, p. 1

This is the heart of the matter, and what Brown sees as concerning "history and verisimilitude". However, as I have made pains to establish, on what foundations is the verisimilitude built if there is no history? Thus the accounts are inspired by trying to develop an "intelligibility" for the reader. These accounts would certainly be full of theological meaning and intelligibility, but then so do stories of pure fiction placed in historical settings. For Brown, it seems that Matthew is all about being both "interesting folklore" and "a salvific message that Matthew could develop harmoniously".

In other words, it never happened as Matthew claimed it did. Jesus may offer salvation, but we cannot derive that truth from these narratives since these narratives seem to contain little or no historical fact.

The final issue to bring up here is one of culpability for the death of innocent children. This is the only moment, it appears, in the New Testament where bad things happening to others are caused directly by the existence of Jesus. With god's will, Jesus is born and thus directly causes (through his existence as intended by God) Herod to murder those innocent babies. God would have known this in advance, and yet still allowed it, and the causal reality is that, in effect, Jesus' birth is responsible for that outcome. Harvey Cox (teacher of a Jesus and morality course, amongst other things, at Harvard) admits in *When Jesus Came to Harvard: Making Moral Choices Today* (2006, p. 81):

> In this case Jesus did, at least indirectly, cause the death of the children of Bethlehem. Ironically, although Christians often say of Jesus "he died for us," in this case, those children died for him.

Perhaps, as David E. Garland (*Reading Matthew: A Literary and Theological Commentary*, 2001, p.179) claims, the Massacre of the Innocents means that in Jesus' own death, "death has been foreshadowed". This seems a rather horrible mechanism for God to use in order to merely "foreshadow" death when it finally comes to Jesus. It is this kind of apologetic contrivance that I find entirely implausible in such contexts. What remains patently the case is that an all-loving God deemed it a perfect choice[1] to design or merely allow for Jesus (himself) to be causally instrumental in the death of a number of innocent babies. Problematically, this still allows God to retain the label of omnibenevolent.

---

[1] All choices from a perfect, omniscient being must, by definition, be perfect.

18 – The Flight to Egypt as a theological mechanism, and as contradicting Luke

As we saw in the last section, in the Old Testament, the account of Moses and his journey in delivering the Hebrews out of Egypt and into the Promised Land is one of the most iconic and key accounts. It was Moses' calling to lead the Hebrew slaves out of captivity in Egypt and into a new and Promised Land, to a new birth of a new culture. If Jesus was to be regarded as the crucial figure he was claimed to be by the Gospel writers and early Christians, then he had some pretty well-respected characters with whom to compete.

This section will follow quite closely the framework of the last section in that the Flight to / from Egypt is part of the Moses narrative and is yet another case of a 'historical' claim being founded on a midrashic reinterpretation of the Old Testament.

Let us be reminded of the relevant extracts from Matthew 2:

> [13] Now when they had gone, behold, an angel of the Lord *appeared to Joseph in a dream and said, "Get up! Take the Child and His mother and flee to Egypt, and remain there until I tell you; for Herod is going to search for the Child to destroy Him."
>
> [14] So Joseph got up and took the Child and His mother while it was still night, and left for Egypt. [15] He remained there until the death of Herod. This was to fulfil what had been spoken by the Lord through the prophet: "OUT OF EGYPT I ALLED MY SON."
>
> ...
>
> [19] But when Herod died, behold, an angel of the Lord *appeared in a dream to Joseph in Egypt, and said, [20] "Get up, take the Child and His mother, and go into the land of Israel; for those who sought the Child's life are dead." [21] So Joseph got up, took the Child and His mother, and came into the land of Israel. [22] But when he heard that Archelaus was reigning over Judea in place of his father Herod, he was afraid to go there. Then after be-

ing warned by God in a dream, he left for the regions of
Galilee, [23] and came and lived in a city called Nazareth. This
was to fulfil what was spoken through the prophets: "He
shall be called a Nazarene."

Straight away, in verse 15, we are given a reason why this
whole episode is contrived: "to fulfil what had been spoken by the
Lord through the prophet". This all happened *so that* a prophecy
could be fulfilled. There seems to be no better reason. As Moses
came out of Egypt, leading his Israelite followers and creating a
new kingdom, so Jesus comes out of Egypt to herald the coming
kingdom of God. Just as God delivers Moses from Egypt, he also
delivers Jesus from Egypt. This revolves around the prophecy
uttered in Hosea 11:1 as referenced in Matthew 2:15.

The meaning of Hosea can be seen in two ways. Firstly, that
Hosea didn't really understand his own words and that they were
obviously understood by God and eventually by Matthew. The
other reading of this would be that it does not refer to Jesus at all
(as Matthew endeavours to set out) but that it merely refers to the
nation of Israel as most obviously read.

Of course, the first and most obvious problem is that this
event of Jesus going to and from Egypt is not corroborated by any
other account. Luke, for example, tells a completely different
story. In Luke, we have Jesus and family moving in a completely
different fashion (Luke 2: 22-24):

> And when eight days had passed, before His circum-
> cision, His name was then called Jesus, the name given by
> the angel before He was conceived in the womb.
>
> And when the days for their purification according
> to the law of Moses were completed, they brought Him up
> to Jerusalem to present Him to the Lord.

It is very clear here that Luke is not giving any spare time
for Joseph and family to have a lengthy two year sojourn in Egypt.
With the use of time connectives such as "when... they..." it follows there is no room for Egypt in any reading of Luke's account.

But not only is the Egyptian saga not mentioned in Luke, it
is simply not referred to in any other New Testament book. If
such a flight to and from Egypt had such strong theological veri-

similitude, then why is it completely ignored by all the other New Testament writers? This is most plausibly explained by realising that the other writers did not know of this since it was developed by Matthew.

There are later, non-canonical texts which detail the time period in Egypt which are important to the Egyptian Coptic Church for obvious reasons. They would have had access to Matthew as a source. However, there is a reason that these texts are not canonical, and as such, they are not seen as historically viable.

Bearing in mind, again, that Matthew's audience was predominantly Jewish, and he was essentially evangelising a risen God-man figure as the Messiah, he had his work cut out to break the conventions of Jewish Messianic figures and realise a deep theological narrative in order to convince such a collective (or appeal to a newly converted collective). This passage fits the bill for doing such things.

Some apologists[1] claim that because it was common for people to, at times, seek 'asylum' in Egypt from the Northwest, then this is a likely account. Of course, this is a non-sequitur. It is not wholly uncommon for people to be assassinated in the world of international politics. This does not mean that Bill Clinton assassinated his associates as proponents of the "Clinton Body Count" conspiracy theory claim. Scientists have created artificial diseases, but this does not mean that AIDS was artificially created by scientists with an agenda as is claimed by some other conspiracy theorists. In order for such claims to be believed, they need to be backed up by solid evidence. In the case of Joseph and family's Flight to Egypt, there is no such evidence outside of a very short and uncorroborated claim which is, in fact, contradicted by the counter-claim of what happened after the birth in Luke's Gospel. As award-winning scholar John Renard expounds in *Islam and Christianity: Theological Themes in Comparative Perspective* (2011, p. 73):

> An example of New Testament narrative based on the Jewish tradition of midrashic exegesis is Matthew's account of the flight into Egypt (Matthew 2:13-15) and the follow-up story of Herod's slaughter of the innocents (Mat-

---

[1] E.g. James Kiefer in "The Infancy Narratives in Matthew and Luke"

thew 2:16-18). Though only Matthew includes these two brief narratives, many Christians choose to believe that they reflect actual historical occurrences—not that attestation in only a single source need in itself cast doubt on their historicity. From the perspective of narrative theology, however, it is essential to take into account that both stories bear the unmistakable stamp of *midrash*, arising out of reflection (*derash*) on, and designed to explain the true meaning of, certain scriptural texts—Old Testament texts in this instance, cited by an author writing for a Jewish audience.

And that, really, is both the Massacre of the Innocents and the Flight to Egypt in a nutshell—not necessarily historically accurate, but midrash to illustrate a theological understanding of Jesus. As ever, the golden question remains: where is the factual evidence which *actually* casts this theological shadow?

Famous Christian apologist N.T. Wright in his article "God's Way of Acting" is far more generous:

> One can challenge the flight into Egypt as simply a back-projection from a fanciful reading of Hosea 11:1. These are the natural probing questions of the historian. As with most ancient history, of course, we cannot verify independently that which is reported only in one source. If that gives grounds for ruling it out, however, most of ancient history goes with it. Let us by all means be suspicious, but let us not be paranoid. Just because I've had a nightmare doesn't mean that there aren't burglars in the house. Just because Matthew says that something fulfilled scripture doesn't mean it didn't happen.

Although the logic here may be sound, he ignores the positive problems that there are with the passage (the contradiction with Luke), the historical issues (was Herod actually alive at the time of the census?) and such like. Simply put, apologists afford the Bible far more charity than it deserves. If these passages were from another holy book, and the same scholars were critiquing it, they would, I wager, come to exactly the same conclusions as non-Christian scholars do of the historicity of these infancy narratives.

19 – The magi and shepherds as evangelists are strangely silent

One substantially important idea that is often overlooked is that both the magi and the shepherds, from the dichotomous positions on the demographic spectrum, simply disappear off the face of the earth (for all intents and purposes) after the birth of Jesus.

This is a vital point since both groups represent incredible opportunities to evangelise the birth and existence of the newly born Messiah. The magi had travelled no doubt their greatest journey, risked their lives and had undergone huge effort just to drop some presents off and praise a baby, whilst the shepherds had witnessed a host of angels (the most incredible thing they would ever see in their lives) and charged off to offer their own praises to the Messiah.

Let us first look at the magi. These three men were obviously rich (since they had fabulous gifts, could afford a massive journey, and had respected 'positions'). Their 'job titles' meant that they were respected within their communities, evidently by the fact that we know them as the Wise Men. With this authority and social standing within their (respective) communities, one would assume that they would be the perfect evangelists for a new-found religion. If, indeed, they experienced what was claimed by Matthew, if they were who they are purported to be, and if they returned home as is stated, then these three wise men would have been in the perfect position to not only record their exploits, but to communicate to a great many others the wonders that they had seen. Either way, one would absolutely expect there to be some record of some type as to what these important figures saw and experienced. Whether their ideas were received with interest and vigour, or whether they were rejected out of hand, there would have been something worth committing to some kind of more permanent record. And yet all we have is a penetrating silence. There is simply nothing of any historical value (if we ignore the overtly mythical claims of the wise men from some later cultures) that can be derived from their existence after leaving Jesus. The key questions are: if these accounts are historically accurate, is this what we would expect and is this probable? The answer to both of these questions is a resounding "no". Is this what we would expect if these events and characters were theological and literary creations? The answer to both of these questions is a resounding "yes". Of course, as with other arguments to debunk the historicity of the nativity, this point does not disprove the historicity in isolation, but lends itself to a cumulative case to dismiss the notion of historicity. It is a game of probability and the dice are loaded in favour of disbelieving such accounts.

In addition to the idea that the magi simply disappeared off the face of the world, recently visited by God incarnate, after meeting said God face-to-face, we also have the problem that the shepherds also disappeared without a trace. This compounds issues of probability. If one is not convinced that well-respected wise men in positions of authority would not make decent evangelists in the name of Jesus, then those at the opposite end of the spectrum could well fit the bill. New Testament scholar with expertise in the socio-demographics of early Christianity James Crossley, in *Why Christianity Happened*, details the socio-economic context in which Christianity arose. He talks in great detail of the importance of entire households converting through social networks such that the richer household owners would convert their servants / slaves and their friends. As he states, "Jesus' view of the law reflected a key aspect of his general teaching: the immense problems that come with socioeconomic inequality" (2006, p. 35). These shepherds at the wrong end of the socio-economic spectrum are the prime target audience for the ministry of Jesus. Luke, writing well after the ministry of Jesus, is sure to have had this in mind when bringing them into the narrative.

Further to this, Crossley continues that "[c]onversion through social networks and affective ties no doubt played a crucial role in the spread of earliest Christianity" (2006, p.144). In order to believe that the accounts of both the magi and the shepherds were factually accurate, one has to discount the idea that the two groups were part of any social network. There seems to be no evidence that they underwent any of the conversion experiences that early Christians did, as according to social scientists.

This is all the more impressive since these two groups of people *experienced first hand* a great deal more, by a substantial margin, than almost *any and every* early Christian, let alone modern evangelisers. In stark contrast to what we might think probable, Associate Professor of Theology Dawn DeVries, in *Jesus Christ in the Preaching of Calvin and Schleiermacher*, proposes that (1996, p. 74) "We do not know what happened to the shepherds after they returned to their flocks. Perhaps they forgot all about what had happened to them." Really? Is that really a viable suggestion? They just forgot the most amazing events that would ever have happened to them, that has ever happened in the last 2,000 years? This is the talk of someone obsessed with the presuppositional authenticity of a group of texts to the point that obvious and probable outcomes are overruled in favour of retaining a literal or authentic message in the name of God.

It simply beggars belief that both groups of people, one visited by a host of angels, another led from foreign lands by a supernatural star before a dangerous king, witness God incarnate, praise the baby, and return to their daily lives of shepherding and stargazing never to be heard from again.

Is this plausible?

20 – Any other business

Now that I have entertained the main reasons for not believing in the historical claims of the infancy narrative of Jesus (if, indeed, they ever were intended to be historical), it is time to look at some other reasons that perhaps don't warrant quite such depth in their analysis.

Firstly, it has been claimed that Herod, being in his 70s at the supposed time of Jesus' birth, would not have been too bothered about chasing after a 'usurper to the throne'. By the time Jesus would have been old enough to trouble Herod's rule, Herod would have known that he himself would be long dead. One might counter this point to say that he still did ruthless things late in his rule and that he may have been thinking of his family who would take over the rule from him. However, on closer inspection, there are problems with such a defence. Indeed, Herod only seemed to do harsh and infamous things late in his rule that would have immediate effect. When he was 70, he installed two golden eagles (Roman symbols) at the temple gates. Two Pharisees, Judas and Mattathias, incited the crowd to a near riot and tore down the eagles, perhaps thinking that Herod was too old to care at this time. Herod burned them alive (see Anthony Tomasino in *Judaism Before Jesus: The Events & Ideas That Shaped the New Testament World*, 2003, p.273). This example shows a vitriolic and intolerant side to Herod but it is clear that this was an action to quell an immediate problem.

Furthermore, Herod left his kingdom in complete turmoil. There seems to be very little evidence of him caring enough about his children and their 'inheritance' for one to conclude anything other than his vicious acts were entirely self-serving and designed for appeal to the present and not the future (of other people). After his death, his kingdom was divided up by Augustus into several parts. As Peter Richardson states in *Herod: King of the Jews and Friend of the Romans*, Herod was at this time "disintegrating and withdrawing from effective participation" in family affairs (1999, p.289). Squabbles followed his death as to who would get what and when. Herod had not got his house in order for it seems it was not high on his list of priorities. So why would catching a newborn and murdering this newborn, thereby forcing him to murder many other infants, be something that such an old king would bother to do? If he could not be bothered to sort out the factions within his own family while he was alive, then why on earth would he be bothered that a usurper, who would only come of age some twenty or so years later and would only eventually grow old enough to take the title of King of the Jews, long after his own death? After all, "Herod's despair was so great over his health problems—he was in his seventieth year and acutely ill—that he tried to kill himself with a paring knife" (Richardson 1999, p.19).

Thus it seems clear that this behaviour from Herod, of reacting so officiously to a prophecy and the magi's news that he murders all the boys under two in Bethlehem and vicinity, is completely out of sorts to what would, in reality, be the behaviour of such a man. Contextual historical evidence shows the purported actions claimed by Matthew to be highly improbable.

A second point to make surrounds Jesus' own family. It appears to be the case that, despite the incredible events surrounding the birth of Jesus, none of his family actually believed he was the Messiah. We know that his brother James did not foster such a belief until after Jesus was crucified (even if this was his true brother). We also know that no one in his hometown believed that he held Messianic properties. Often known as the Rejection of Jesus, all the Synoptic Gospels (though the saying is repeated in John) recount an event whereby Jesus was shunned in his hometown (Nazareth) and, as such, could not carry out any miracles. Jesus goes on to say the amazing words (Matthew 13:57), "A prophet is not without honor except in his hometown and in his own household." Thus it is explicitly reported, from the mouth of Jesus himself, that his hometown and his family rejected him. Even given the possibility that Joseph had died, what could have possessed Mary, with her annunciation and witnessing of an angel, visitation from magi and shepherds, having a star stop over her house and so on, what could possibly have possessed her to doubt the Messianic qualities of her son?

Now many theologians have tried to make sense of this but what certainly remains is a situation whereby people who have witnessed, or have had access to such sources of witness to, an incredible and miraculous event still doubt the implications of such an event. What would best make sense of this? It certainly appears to me that the most sensible option is that the original and miraculous birth events never took place (including the annunciations not particularly investigated here). If the events were not actual historical events, then the reaction of the hometown and the family is much more easily explicable.

A third point regards the confusion that exists in the language surrounding the word 'Nazareth'. As Hayyim ben Yehoshua in an online essay, *Refuting Missionaries*, says[1]:

> But why did the Christians believe that he lived in Nazareth? The answer is quite simple. The early Greek speaking Christians did not know what the word "Nazarene" meant. The earliest Greek form of this word is "Nazoraios," which is derived from "Natzoriya," the Aramaic equivalent of the Hebrew "Notzri." (Recall that "Yeishu ha-Notzri" is the original Hebrew for "Jesus the Nazarene.") The early Christians conjectured that "Nazarene" meant a person from Nazareth and so it was assumed that Jesus lived in Nazareth. Even today, Christians blithely confuse the Hebrew words "Notzri" (*Nazarene, Christian*), "Natzrati" (*Nazarethite*) and "nazir" (*nazarite*), all of which have completely different meanings.

There have been various claims that the town of Nazareth was uninhabited at the time of Jesus birth and was only later inhabited, predominantly at the time that the Gospel writers would have been writing their accounts of Jesus' life. One such proponent is René Salm who conducted extensive secondary research into the archaeology and history of the town of Nazareth and wrote *The Myth of Nazareth* to put forward this thesis.

Salm's conclusion is that the settlement did not come into existence any earlier than 70 CE. He claims that it was uninhabited from around 700 BCE to around 100 CE. He arrived at this conclusion by looking at archaeological findings from excavations in the area which unanimously provide glass, metal, oil lamps, inscriptions, coins and such like as well as building foundations

---

[1] http://mama.indstate.edu/users/nizrael/jesusrefutation.html (retrieved 16/02/2012)

and similar evidence. The oil lamps are of particular interest to Salm as they represent the earliest evidence and he deems these artefacts as being Herodian in chronology.

Salm makes much of the Nazareth claims from inside the Gospels. Mark only references Nazareth once (1:9) which Salm claims was likely an interpolation (other references in Mark are to Jesus the Nazarene rather than Jesus being from *Nazaret*[1]). Otherwise Mark claims Jesus is from Capernaum, stating he is at home there and that his family live there. He makes no mention of them ever moving from Nazareth to Capernaum. In Matthew 2:22-3 the author states "he left for the regions of Galilee, and came and lived in a city called Nazareth. *This was* to fulfil what was spoken through the prophets: 'He shall be called a Nazarene.'" The issue here is that no one knows of this prophecy—it is not in the Old Testament or any other literature. Salm sees Luke as reacting against Capernaum claims, that Capernaum was actually where he was from. R.T. France in *The Gospel of Matthew* (2007, p. 92-93) illustrates that Nazorean (Nazarene) and Nazirite (a cult to which Samson belonged in Judges) are only one letter different in the original Greek. This could be responsible for some of the confusion. Therefore, there could well have been confusion in the understanding of what Nazorean meant with an early understanding being a sort of religious title but that it was later interpreted to refer to a town. But Salm suggests this town did not, in its Galilean site, exist at Jesus' time.

Early Christian writers seem to avoid mentioning Nazareth and show no evidence that they know where it is and indeed illustrate confusion over the matter (Salm 2008, p.294-9). Importantly, despite what one might expect, there is no record of any kind of pilgrimage up to the 4th century CE. The earliest mention outside of the New Testament is by Julius Africanus in about 200 CE. The confusion generally reflects two different approaches: the southern, Judean Nazareth and the northern, Galilean Nazareth. There were, it seems, possibly two Nazareths. Luke claims that Nazareth is on the "brow of a hill" (4:29). This makes more sense of a southern claim to Nazareth in Judea.

---

[1] It is referred to variously as *Nazara, Nazaret* and *Nazareth*. The fact that Mark has all three spellings lends evidence to the theory that Mark was written by different hands or at different stages.

Christian archaeologists have known that there has been no real indication from in and around Nazzareth that it was inhabited at the time of the birth of Jesus, which is why an archaeological discovery in Nazareth that supposedly dates from the period was heralded so gleefully by apologists in 2009. This is how the BBC reported it[1]:

> Archaeologists in Israel say they have uncovered the remains of the first dwelling in Nazareth believed to date back to the time of Jesus Christ...
>
> A spokeswoman said Jesus and his childhood friends likely knew the home...
>
> The archaeologists found the remains of a wall, a hideout, and a cistern for collecting rain water.

Now, given that this evidence stands, then we can see that the Myth of Nazareth theory adhered to by the likes of Salm falls apart. However, things aren't so simple. Surrounding this claim were some very suspicious circumstances. Firstly, the dig was being carried out by the Catholic Church in order to make way for the Mary of Nazareth International Center. This bias, of course, does not mean that the dig is suspect a priori but the rest of these points do:

- The archaeologist Yardenna Alexandre has not published any of the findings or verified any of the claims.
- No one else has done so either.
- The Israel Antiquities Authority published a short statement, only to take it off the web soon after.
- The Church remains the only port of call for verifying the claims.
- The Church (rather conveniently) proceeded to build over the remains meaning it can never be verified.
- No materials exist in any scholarly record.

---

[1]"Jesus-era home found in Nazareth",
http://news.bbc.co.uk/1/hi/8425094.stm (retrieved 16/03/2012)

- In the Catholic Literature, this was admitted: "Up till then [that is, the recent 'house' discovery], there was no scientific evidence affirming the existence of a village of Nazareth of the epoch of Christ."[1] This is an explicit admission that there is, apart from this so-called discovery, no evidence to support Nazareth being inhabited at the time of Jesus.

This interests me more than his main thesis in all honesty, since it clearly shows the levels to which the Catholic Church (or any religious organisation) are willing to go to support their worldview. These points make the entire house claim thoroughly dubious. We have no evidence, just the word of an archaeologist employed by the Catholic Church. The evidence has since been destroyed, it seems, without any independent and professional corroboration. Furthermore, the admission of the Church that there is no other evidence to support an inhabited Nazareth is a massive concession.

I remain agnostic as to whether Nazareth existed or was inhabited at the time of Jesus. There are certainly interesting arguments either way. What we do have confusion over, indubitably, is seen in the tradition which sees Jesus as a Nazorean who came from Capernaum and whose connection to Nazareth was a later correction, either mistakenly or with an agenda in mind. The devil is in the detail and the detail is murky.

---

[1] René Salm on his website http://www.nazarethmyth.info/scandalsix (retrieved 16/03/2012).

Conclusion

After such an analysis, what conclusions can be drawn? It seems clear to me that the claims of the two Gospels, Matthew and Luke, are incredibly problematic. On the surface, it seems fairly obvious to vouch that one narrative must be wrong (at the very least) in order to allow one to remain intact and coherent. However, this does not go far enough. It seems perfectly evident that neither of the accounts stand up to critical scrutiny, even if taken in isolation. Using extra-biblical sources, but more importantly, probability and plausibility, we can conclude that the infancy narratives almost certainly did not occur, certainly in the manner in which is claimed by the Gospel writers. The literal understanding of the biblical birth narratives is not sustainable.

In order for the Christian who believes that both accounts are factually true to uphold that faithful decree, the following steps must take place. The believer must:

- Special plead that the virgin birth motif *is actually* true for Christianity but is false for all other religions and myths that claim similarly.
- Deny that "virgin" is a mistranslation.
- Give a plausible explanation of from whence the male genome of Jesus came from and how this allowed him to be "fully man".
- Be able to render the two genealogies fully coherent without the explanation being contrived or ad hoc.
- Believe that the genealogies are bona fide and not just tools to try to prove Jesus' Davidic and Messianic prophecy-fulfilling heritage.
- Be able to explain the inconsistency of the two accounts in contradicting each other as to where Jesus' family lived before the birth (without the explanation being contrived or ad hoc).
- Somehow be able to contrive an explanation whereby Herod and Quirinius could be alive con-

currently, despite all the evidence contrary to this point.

- Believe that a client kingdom under Herod could and would order a census under Roman diktat. This would be the only time in history this would have happened.
- Find it plausible that people would return, and find precedent for other occurrences of people returning, to their ancestral homes for a census (at an arbitrary number of generations before: 41).
- Give a probable explanation as to how a Galilean man was needed at a census in another judicial area.
- Give a plausible reason as to why Mary was required at the census (by the censors or by Joseph).
- Give a plausible explanation as to why Mary would make that 80 mile journey on donkey or on foot whilst heavily pregnant, and why Joseph would be happy to let her do that.
- Believe that Joseph could afford to take anywhere from a month to two years off work.
- Believe that, despite archaeological evidence, Nazareth existed as a proper settlement at the time of Jesus' birth.
- Believe that the prophecies referred to Nazareth and not something else.
- Believe that the magi were not simply a theological tool derived from the Book of Daniel.
- Believe that Herod (and his scribes and priests) was not acting entirely out of character and implausibly in not knowing the prophecies predicting Jesus, and not accompanying the magi three hours down the road.
- Believe that the magi weren't also merely a mechanism to supply Herod with an opportunity to get involved in the story and thus fulfil even more prophecies.
- Believe that the magi were also not a reinterpretation of the Balaam narrative from the Old

Testament, despite there being clear evidence to the contrary.

- Believe that a star could lead some magi from the East to Jerusalem and then to Bethlehem where it rested over an individual house and not be noted by anyone else in the world.
- Believe that the shepherds were not merely midrashic and theological tools used by Luke.
- Believe that there is (and provide it) a reasonable explanation as to why each Gospel provides different first witnesses (shepherds and magi) without any mention of the other witnesses.
- Believe that, despite an absence of evidence and the realisation that it is clearly a remodelling of an Old Testament narrative, the Massacre of the Innocents actually happened.
- Believe that Herod would care enough about his rule long after his death to chase after a baby and murder many other innocent babies, a notion that runs contrary to evidence.
- Believe that God would allow other innocent babies to die as a result of the birth of Jesus.
- Believe that the Flight to and from Egypt was not just a remodelling of an Old Testament narrative in order to give Jesus theological gravitas.
- Give a plausible explanation as to why the two accounts contradict each other so obviously as to where Jesus and family went after his birth.
- Explain the disappearance of the shepherds and magi, who had seen the most incredible sights of their lives, and why they are never heard from again despite being the perfect spokespeople for this new-found religion.
- Provide a plausible explanation as to why Jesus' own family did not think he was the Messiah, given the events of the nativity accounts.

Once the believer in the accuracy of these accounts can do all of the above, in a plausible and probable manner, then they can rationally hold that belief. I would contest that it is rationally possible to ever hold such a belief.

But does a Christian have to hold the belief that *all* of the claims are true? This is something which I have mentioned several times. The difficulty here for such a (liberal) Christian is how to arrive at any kind of a rational basis as to what they accept and what they reject. Given that it has been shown that every single claim can be soundly doubted under critical examination, it is difficult to build a case for any veracity within the combined, two-prong approach of the infancy narratives. There really is no solid rational foundation to an acceptance that, for example, the virgin birth claims are true, but the magi are probably false; or that the magi were real and factual, but the star was not; or that the shepherd encounter truly happened as reported, but that the census never took place. It would be fairly arbitrary at best. Many of the events are crucially interconnected.

The ramifications for pulling the rug out from under the believers' feet is that we are left with no proper account of Jesus' life until, really, he starts his ministry. Furthermore, we have no real evidence for the claims that Jesus is the Messiah and is derived from Messianic and Davidic heritage. As a result, we have only the accounts of the miraculous events surrounding Jesus' ministry and death. However, the same problems afflict these accounts: they are uncorroborated by extra-biblical, non pro-Jesus attestation and rely on unknown authors writing in unknown places. What is particularly damaging, as I have already set out, is that if the birth narratives can be shown to be patently false, and the narratives involve sizeable accounts from two Gospel writers, then how can we know what other purported facts are true? If these infancy miracle claims are false, then what of the myriad of other miracle claims—the walking on the water, the water to wine, the resurrection? It is a serious indictment of these writers (especially since Luke is declared as being a reliable historian by so many apologists[1]).

The undermining of these narratives does not disprove that Jesus was the Son of God, or that he had Davidic lineage, or what-

---

[1] It is worth referring you to another work of Richard Carrier, *Not the Impossible Faith*, which does an excellent job of dispelling this ubiquitous assertion.

ever else these passages were trying to establish, per se. However, one has to recognise that some really damaging chinks are undoubtedly beaten into the apologetic armour of claims of Jesus' divinity.

So while I have not proved anything entirely (in a Cartesian manner, what can be entirely 'proved' other than I exist?), I believe that I have provided a cumulative case which is overwhelmingly decisive in showing that the infancy narratives are almost certainly non-historical. As a result, it then follows that the rational belief in the divinity of Jesus, if based on such historical evidence in any way, then becomes equally damaged. Because these claims involve events which can be investigated in some way using existing sources outside of the Bible, we are in a more historically verifiable position to analyse these narratives. Other passages in the biographical accounts of Jesus' life are not afforded such verifiability, unfortunately. As such, the assertions of the rest of the Gospels are taken on their own merits rather than allowing historians to be able to see if they match up with extra-biblical evidence.

As apologist Jason Engwer on influential Christian internet site "triablogue" asserts after investigating many theological and historical analyses of the nativity:

> It seems that the early Christian and non-Christian consensus that viewed the infancy narratives as historical accounts was correct. Whether those historical accounts about Jesus' infancy were accurate is another issue ... but the accounts were meant to convey history.[1]

So there are theists (indeed, many) who certainly *do* believe it is *indeed* an attempt at history, and not just theology dressed up as history. Catholic Tarcisio Beal in *Foundations of Christianity: The Historical Jesus and His World* (2009, p. 123-4) in referring to the work of Richard A. Horsley, argues that the history of the narratives is rooted in the very real context in which they are set— one of "Roman and Herodian oppression":

---

[1] http://triablogue.blogspot.com/2006/11/were-infancy-narratives-meant-to.html (retrieved 07/03/2012)

The heavy burden of taxation, not historical accuracy, is the main point of the census of Quirinius ...

Thus, the story of the "Massacre of the Innocent" is rooted in the historical reality of Palestine at the time of Jesus' birth. No, it did not happen the way Matthew tells us or some other contemporary sources would have mentioned it.

This is pitted against Engwer's approach, and both are Christians. I would agree with Beal, but would add crucially that while the context may well be true, this has absolutely no bearing on the claims to a historical Jesus.

New Zealand biblical scholar and philosopher Gregory Dawes in *The Historical Jesus Question: the Challenge for History to Religious Authority* (2001, p.301) affirms:

> It shows us that the early Christians were so keen to demonstrate that the *kerygma* had a historical grounding that, where necessary, they were prepared to invent an appropriate history... As Käsemann writes, "Matthew no longer has any doubt that he is recapitulating genuine history."[1] By handing on what we would judge to be a fictitious history, Matthew unwittingly bears witness to how much he valued historical facts.

Which brings us back round to the doubting of the other [Matthew's] historical claims within the Gospels. Therefore, it appears that no matter which tack an apologist takes, whether to defend a historical reliability or a purely theological one, the nature of the evident deconstruction of the infancy narratives undermines any rational defence of the infancy narratives (and, to an extent, the Gospel accounts as a whole) embodying some sort of truth.

---

[1] Dawes references German biblical scholar Ernst Käsemann's famous essay "The Problem of the Historical Jesus", p.26.

BIBLIOGRAPHY

Books:

Albright, William and Mann, C.S. (1971), *The Anchor Bible. Matthew*, New York: Doubleday

Alter, Robert and Kermode, Frank (1990), *The Literary Guide to the Bible*, Harvard: Harvard University Press

Barens, E.W (1947), *The Rise of Christianity*, London: Longmans, Green

Beal, Tarcisio (2009), *Foundations of Christianity: The Historical Jesus and His World*, Bloomingtom, IN: AuthorHouse

Brown, Raymond (1977), *The Birth of the Messiah*, London: Geoffrey Chapman

Brown, Raymond (1997), *Introduction to the New Testament.* New York: Anchor Bible

Burkett, Delbert (2002), *An Introduction To The New Testament And The Origins Of Christianity*, Cambridge: Cambridge University Press.

Burnett, A.M. (1992), *Roman Provincial Coinage*, London: British Museum Press

Callahan, Tim (2002), *The Secret Origins of the Bible*, Altadena: Millennium Press

Campbell, Patrick (1965), *The Mythical Jesus*, Waverley

Carrier, Richard (2009), *Not the Impossible Faith*, lulu.com

Cline, E.H. (2009), *Biblical Archaeology: A Very Short Introduction (Very Short Introductions)*, OUP USA

Cohen, S.J.D. (1979), *Josephus in Galilee and Rome, his Vita and Development as a Historian*, Leiden: E.J. Brill

Conybeare, Fred Cornwallis (2nd Ed 1910; reprint 2010), *Myths, Magic and Morals*, Whitefish, MT: Kessinger Publishing

Corley, Jeremy (2009), *New Perspectives on the Nativity*, London: T & T Clark International

Cox, Harvey (2006), *When Jesus Came to Harvard: Making Moral Choices Today*, New York: Mariner Books

Craveri, Marcello (1967), *The Life of Jesus*, London: Secker & Warburg (RandomHouse)

Crossley, James G. (2006), *Why Christianity Happened*, Louisville, Kentucky: Westminster John Knox Press

Crossan, John Dominic (1999), *The Birth of Christianity*, New York: HarperOne

Dabrowa, Edward (1998), *The Governors of Roman Syria from Augustus to Septimius Severus*, Germany: R. Habelt

DeVries, Dawn (1996), *Jesus Christ in the Preaching of Calvin and Schleiermacher*, Louisville, Kentucky: Westminster John Knox Press

Davies, William David and Allison, Dale C., (2nd ed 2000), *A critical and exegetical commentary on the Gospel according to Saint Matthew: in three volumes. Introduction and commentary on Matthew 1-VII, Volume 1*, London: T & T Clark

Davis, Mike (2008), *The Atheist's Guide to the New Testament*, Denver: Outskirts Press

Dawes, Gregory W. (2001), *The Historical Jesus Question: the Challenge for History to Religious Authority*, Louisville, Kentucky: Westminster John Knox Press

Elder, John (1960), *Prophets, Idols, and Diggers: Scientific Proof of Bible History*, New York: Bobbs Merrill Co.

Eusebius of Caesarea, Tr. W.J. Ferrar (1920), *Demonstratio Evangelica* (http://www.tertullian.org/fathers/eusebius_de_00_epref ace.htm)

Evans, Craig A. (2003), *The Bible Knowledge Background Commentary: Matthew-Luke*, Colorado: Victor (Cook Communications Ministries)

Finegan, Jack (1998; rev. Ed), *Handbook of Biblical Chronology*, Peabody, MA: Hendrickson Publishers

Fitzgerald, David (2010), *Nailed: Ten Christian Myths That Show Jesus Never Existed at All*, Lulu.com

Foster, Charles (2007), *The Christmas Mystery*, Milton Keynes: Authentic Media

France, R.T. (2007), *The Gospel of Matthew (New International Commentary on the New Testament)*, Grand Rapids, MI: Wm. B. Eerdmans Publishing Co.

Garland, David E. (2001), *Reading Matthew: A Literary and Theological Commentary*, Macon, Georgie: Smyth & Helwys Publishing Inc.

Garner, Jane F. (1991), *Women in Roman Law and Society*, UK: First Midland

Green, Joel B. (1997), *The Gospel of Luke*, Grand Rapids: Wm. B. Eerdmans Publishing Co.

Guignebert, Charles (1935), *Jesus*, London: Kegan Paul

Hinnells, John R. (2010), *The Routledge Companion to the Study of Religion*, Oxon: Routledge

Jackson, Samuel Macauley Ed. (1953), *The New Schaff-Herzog Encyclopedia of Religious Knowledge, Vol. VI: Innocents - Liudger*, Grand Rapids, Michigan: Baker Book House

Josephus, *Jewish War*, translation referenced at http://perseus.uchicago.edu/perseus-cgi/citequery3.pl?dbname=GreekTexts&query=Joseph.%20BJ&getid=1 using the Perseus Digital Library at Tufts

Köster, Helmut (2004), *Ancient Christian Gospels: their History and Development*, Harrisburg, PA: Trinity Press International

Kraus, S. (1904), "Jesus of Nazareth", *The Jewish Encyclopaedia*, New York: Funk & Wagnalls

Lachs, Samuel Tobias (1987), *A Rabbinic Commentary on the New Testament: The Gospels of Matthew, Mark and Luke*, Ktav Publishing House, Incorporated

Larson, Martin A., (1989), *The Essene-Christian Faith*, Truth Seeker Co Inc

McRay, John (1991), *Archaeology and the New Testament*, MI: Baker Book House

Martin, Ernest, L. (1991; 2nd ed), *The Star that Astonished the World*, Portland: Associates for Scriptural Knowledge

Mason, Steve (1992) "Josephus and Luke-Acts," *Josephus and the New Testament*, Peabody, Massachusetts: Hendrickson Publishers

Millar, Fergus (1995), *The Roman Near East: 31 BC-AD 337*, Harvard: Harvard University Press

Nabarz, Payam (2005), *The mysteries of Mithras: The Pagan Belief That Shaped The Christian World*, Rochester, VT: Inner Traditions

Nicolet, Claude (1976) translated by Falla, P.S. (1980), *The World of the Citizen in Republican Rome*, Berkeley: University of California Press

159

O'Leary, D.L. (1912), *Studies in the Apocryphal Gospels of Christ's Infancy*, London: Robert Sutton

Pearce, Jonathan M.S. (2010), *Free Will? An investigation into whether we have free will or whether I was always going to write this book*, Hampshire: Ginger Prince Publications

Price, Robert M. (2003), *Incredible Shrinking Son of Man: How Reliable Is the Gospel Tradition?*, Armherst, NY: Prometheus Books

Racy, Richard (2007), *Nativity*, Authorhouse

Ranke-Heinemann, Uta (1995), *Putting Away Childish Things*, San Francisco: HarperSanFrancisco

Renard, John (2011), *Islam and Christianity: Theological Themes in Comparative Perspective*, Berkley: University of California Press

Richardson, Peter (1999), *Herod: King of the Jews and Friend of the Romans*, Edinburgh: T & T Clark Ltd

Salm, René (2008), *The Myth of Nazareth*, Parisppany, NJ: American Atheist Press

Spong, John Shelby (1997), *Liberating the Gospels: Reading the Bible with Jewish Eyes*, San Francisco: HarperSanFrancisco

Stark, Thom (2011), *The Human Face of God: What Scripture Reveals When It Gets God Wrong (And Why Inerrancy Tries To Hide It)*, Eugene, OR: Wipf & Stock Publishers

Stein, Robert H. (1993), *Luke: The New American Commentary*, B & H Publishing Group

Strauss, D.F. (4th Ed 1860) translated by Evans, Marian, *The Life of Jesus*, New York: Calvin Blanchard

Strobel, Lee (1998), *The Case for Christ: A Journalist's Personal Investigation of the Evidence for Jesus*, Grand Rapids, MI: Zondervan

Summers, Ray and Vardaman, Jerry E. (1998), *Chronos Kairos Christos II*, Macon: Mercer University Press

Tabor, James (2007), *The Jesus Dynasty: The Hidden History of Jesus, His Royal Family, and the Birth of Christianity*, New York: Simon & Schuster

Theissen, G., Merz, A (1998 trans. Bowden, J.), *The Historical Jesus : A Comprehensive Guide*, Fortress Press

160

Tomasino, Anthony J. (2003), *Judaism Before Jesus: The Events & Ideas That Shaped the New Testament World*, Westmont, Illinois: IVP Academic

Vardaman, Jerry E. and Yamauchi, Edwin M. (1989), *Chronos, Kairos, Christos: Nativity and Chronological Studies Presented to Jack Finegan*, Winona Lake: Eisenbrauns

Vermes, Geza (2006), *The Nativity: History and Legend*, London: Penguin

Essays, papers and articles:

Browning. W. R. F. (1997), "infancy narratives" A Dictionary of the Bible. Retrieved February 21, 2012 from Encyclopedia.com:http://www.encyclopedia.com/doc/1O94-infancynarratives.html

Carrier, Richard (2000), "Luke and Josephus", http://www.infidels.org/library/modern/richard_carrier/l ukeandjosephus.html

Carrier, Richard (2006, 6th Ed.), "Why I Don't Buy the Resurrection Story"
http://www.infidels.org/library/modern/richard_carrier/r esurrection/2.html

Carrier, Richard (2011, 6th Ed.), "The Date of the Nativity in Luke",
http://www.infidels.org/library/modern/richard_carrier/q uirinius.html

Franz, Gordon (2009), "The Slaughter Of The Innocents—Historical Fact Or Legendary Fiction?", *Associates for Biblical Research*,
http://www.biblearchaeology.org/post/2009/12/08/The-Slaughter-of-the-Innocents-Historical-Fact-or-Legendary-Fiction.aspx#Article

Gardner, Martin (1999), "The Star of Bethlehem", *The Skeptical Inquirer Volume 23.6, November / December 1999*

Isbell, Charles D. (June 1977), "Does the Gospel of Matthew Proclaim Mary's Virginity?". *Biblical Archaeological Review 3*

Jenkins, R.M. (2004). "The Star of Bethlehem and the Comet of AD 66". *Journal of the British Astronomy Association* (114): pp. 336–43, June 2004

Jensen, Robin M. (2010), "Witnessing the Divine: The Magi in Art and Literature, *Biblical archaeology Review*, Jan/Feb 2010 E-Feature, http://www.bib-arch.org/e-features/witnessing-divine.asp

Käsemann, Ernst (1954), "The Problem of the Historical Jesus"

Kiefer, James, "The Infancy Narratives in Matthew and Luke", Online essay, Part 2 found here: http://elvis.rowan.edu/~kilroy/christia/library/infancy2.html

Lendering, Jona, "King Herod the Great", http://www.livius.org/he-hg/herodians/herod_the_great01.html

MacGregor, Kirk R., "Is the New Testament Historically Accurate?" (No longer available online at the time of publishing)

Marchant, Ronald (1980), "THE CENSUS OF QUIRINIUS: The Historicity of Luke 2:1-5", IBRI Research Report #4

Miller, Glenn (1999, ed 2008), "On an objection about Luke, Quirinius, and Herods:", http://christianthinktank.com/quirinius.html

Miller, Glenn, "Response to..."The Fabulous Prophecies of the Messiah"", http://christianthinktank.com/fabrach.html

Morris, Henry M., "When They Saw the Star", *Institute for Creation Research*, http://www.icr.org/home/resources/resources_tracts_whentheysawthestar/

Mulholland, Robert M. (1981), "The Infancy Narratives in Matthew and Luke—Of History, Theology and Literature", *Biblical Archaeology Review 7:02, Mar/Apr 1981*

Plait, Phil (2007), "The (bah) Star of (humbug) Bethlehem", *The Discover Magazine, Bad Astronomy*, http://blogs.discovermagazine.com/badastronomy/2007/12/25/the-bah-star-of-humbug-bethlehem/

Price, Robert M. (2004), "New Testament Narrative as Old Testament Midrash" http://www.robertmprice.mindvendor.com/art_midrash1.htm

Rao, Joe (2011), "Was the Star of Bethlehem a star, comet ... or miracle?", *Space on MSNBC.com*, http://www.msnbc.msn.com/id/45778305/ns/technology_and_science-space/t/was-star-bethlehem-star-comet-or-miracle/#.TzUZ5lxNsuM

Steinmann, Andrew E. (2009), "When did Herod the Great reign?", Novum Testamentum, Volume 51, Number 1, 2009, pp. 1-29

Still, James, "The Virgin Birth and Childhood Mysteries of Jesus", http://www.infidels.org/library/modern/james_still/virgin_birth.html#9

Syme, Ronald (1984), "The Titulus Tiburtinus", *Roman Papers*, vol. 3, Anthony Birley, ed.,

Wright, NT (1998), "God's Way of Acting", *The Christian Century*, December 16, 1998, pp. 1215-17

ben Yehoshua, Hayyim, "Refuting Missionaries—Part 1: The Myth of the Historical Jesus", variously, e.g. http://mama.indstate.edu/users/nizrael/jesusrefutation.html

Lightning Source UK Ltd.
Milton Keynes UK
UKOW02f0723101216

289574UK00001B/86/P